Dr Rob Willson, PhD, is a cognitive behavioural therapist in private practice, an author and a researcher based in North London. He has been involved in treating individuals with health anxiety for the past twenty-five years. Rob regularly teaches on the psychological treatment of health anxiety and supervises numerous therapists who specialise in treating the condition. He is a chair of the charity the Body Dysmorphic Disorder Foundation. His website is www.robwillson.com

Professor David Veale is a consultant psychiatrist in cognitive behavioural therapy. He leads a national service for people with anxiety disorders at the South London and Maudsley Trust and also works in private practice. He is a visiting professor at the Institute of Psychiatry, Psychology and Neuroscience, King's College London. He was a member of the group that wrote the NICE guidelines on OCD in 2006, and chaired the NICE Evidence Update on OCD in 2013. He is an Honorary Fellow of the British Association of Behavioural and Cognitive Psychotherapies (BABCP), and fellow both of the British Psychological Society and of the Royal College of Psychiatrists. He is a trustee of the charities OCD Action, the BDD Foundation and Emetophobia Action. His website is www.veale.co.uk

T0004311

The aim of the **Overcoming** series is to enable people with a range of common problems and disorders to take control of their own recovery programme.

Each title, with its specially tailored programme, is devised by a practising clinician using the latest techniques of cognitive behavioural therapy – techniques that have been shown to be highly effective in changing the way patients think about themselves and their problems.

Many books in the Overcoming series are recommended under the Reading Well scheme.

OVERCOMING HEALTH ANXIETY

2nd Edition

*A self-help guide using
cognitive behavioural techniques*

OVERCOMING

ROB WILLSON AND DAVID VEALE

ROBINSON

ROBINSON

First published in Great Britain in 2009 by Robinson,
an imprint of Constable & Robinson Ltd

This revised and updated edition published by Robinson in 2022

1 3 5 7 9 10 8 6 4 2

IMPORTANT NOTE
This book is not intended as a substitute for medical advice or treatment.
Any person with a condition requiring medical attention should consult a
qualified medical practitioner or suitable therapist.

A CIP catalogue record for this book
is available from the British Library.

ISBN: 978-1-47214-660-1

Typeset in Bembo by Initial Typesetting Services, Edinburgh
Printed and bound in Great Britain by Clays Ltd, Elcograf S.p.A.

Papers used by Robinson are from well-managed forests
and other responsible sources.

Robinson
An imprint of
Little, Brown Book Group
Carmelite House
50 Victoria Embankment
London EC4Y 0DZ

An Hachette UK Company
www.hachette.co.uk

www.littlebrown.co.uk

Contents

Acknowledgements

We would like to acknowledge all of the individuals who have health anxiety with whom we have worked. You have taught us much about this challenging problem and are the inspiration for writing this book. We would like to acknowledge all the clinicians and researchers who have contributed to the psychological understanding and treatment of health anxiety. A far from exhaustive list of these includes Paul Salkovskis, Mark Freeston, Ann Hackmann, Peter Tyrer, Paul Gilbert, Steven Taylor, Gordon Asmundonson and David M. Clark.

1

What is health anxiety and how can it be overcome?

The book is for individuals with distressing and persistent anxiety about their health, and for their families and others who care for them. Health anxiety is a common condition in which the person often finds themselves worrying excessively about being ill. For some, this is focused on trying to avoid (or detect early) an illness they particularly fear or dread. For others, this can take the form of a belief that they already have a feared disease, but it has not yet been diagnosed. If you have health anxiety, often this fear persists even if you have been reassured by a doctor that they do not believe that you have that disease. Some people with health anxiety fear the notion of becoming ill in general, and others might fear specific conditions (that may change over time).

As well as experiencing significant distress, people with health anxiety may feel compelled to over-monitor and check for signs of disease. They may also be driven to gather considerable information about health and illness, often from the internet. There are individuals who seek repeated medical reassurance and others who avoid seeing a doctor.

As authors, we are both clinicians and researchers with, between us, over sixty years' experience helping people with health anxiety. In this book we hope to help you understand health anxiety more fully, and to guide you through some tried and tested steps so that you can overcome the problem or support someone else to do so.

What is health anxiety?

Common worries in health anxiety are focused on cancer or serious neurological conditions like multiple sclerosis. You can also be physically ill (for example, have heart disease) but the concerns about the condition are regarded as excessive. Health anxiety is not restricted to physical illness and can include a fear of developing a mental illness like schizophrenia or dementia.

Health anxiety often includes the following features:

- A persistent belief that you have, or a fear about having, one or more serious, life-altering, progressive or life-threatening illnesses. You might believe that you already have your dreaded illness, or you may be more preoccupied by the idea that you *might* (or even that you inevitably will) get it. The belief or fear of having a serious illness are different presentations and have implications for the way you understand the problem.

- The problem will persist despite (or partly because of) a medical examination or reassurance from a doctor. However, please note that it's also not unusual for some people with health anxiety to actively avoid doctors and hospitals.
- A tendency to misinterpret some normal bodily experiences as a sign of disease.
- Checking or monitoring your body for signs of your feared disease(s).
- Checking the internet for information related to your feared disease(s).
- You may fear that you might 'miss something important', like a feature of illness that you should tell a doctor about.
- If you have more of a fear of doubts or uncertainty about your health, then you are likely to be checking your body for evidence of illness. For example, feeling for lumps or scrutinising skin blemishes, spending very large amounts of time searching for information about your feared illness, and repeatedly seeking reassurance and investigations.
- If you strongly believe that you already have a serious physical illness, like cancer, you are more likely to be seeking medical help to investigate or treat the problem. You may be more likely to dismiss any psychological understanding of the problem. Sometimes the belief is so strongly held it is regarded as 'delusional'.
- Unhelpful avoidance behaviour related to health, such as avoiding medical appointments or avoiding

things that trigger your worries like exercise or physical touch.

- Health anxiety often fluctuates in severity and can recur in discrete episodes throughout your lifetime. The content of your fear may also change over time too. For example, your fear may have been focused on AIDS when you were younger, then five years later it was on cancer and now it is on dementia.

The result is significant distress and it's likely you will more easily become worried about the state of your health than average. Your anxiety or related behaviours are likely to be having a serious impact on all important areas of your life, including personal, family, social, educational and occupational.

Hypochondriasis

The original term for persistent fears of illness was 'hypochondriasis' or 'hypochondriacal disorder', but we will not use it in this book since it has developed negative associations. It's important to remember that the cliché of someone with health anxiety constantly calling their doctor for an appointment does not hold true; some people with the problem will excessively *avoid* contact with doctors (because they fear the worst).

The term 'hypochondria' is derived from Greek and literally means 'below the cartilage'. This is because it was thought, at one time, that a problem in the guts of a person caused various mental disorders. In the nineteenth century, hypochondria acquired its more specific meaning of fear of disease and preoccupation with your health. More recently, in the USA, severe and persistent anxiety about your health has been called *Illness Anxiety Disorder* (IAD), but we've stuck with the term health anxiety in this book as it is the term most commonly accepted.

Sometimes the fear of becoming ill is driven by a fear of death, which we discuss in more detail later in this book. For others, the fear is motivated by the idea of suffering forever and not being in control.

Health anxiety can overlap with other common clinical problems such as depression, obsessive-compulsive disorder (OCD), generalised anxiety disorder (GAD) and panic disorder or medically unexplained symptoms. We'll give some more information on these problems below.

Extra problems with health anxiety

People with health anxiety often have other problems, which may make health anxiety harder to treat or to separate out.

Depression and shame

The most common condition accompanying health anxiety is depression. Everybody feels down from time to time, but in normal circumstances the feeling usually passes quickly and doesn't interfere too much with the way we live our lives. When most people say 'I'm depressed' they mean that they are feeling low or sad or perhaps stressed, which are normal facets of human experience. However, when health professionals talk of depression, they are using the term in a different way. They are referring to a condition that is different from the normal ups and downs of everyday life. This is the type of depression we will be discussing: it is more painful than a normal low, lasts longer and interferes with life in all sorts of ways.

Have I got depression?

So how can you tell if you are experiencing depression or just going through a period of feeling low? Depression can only be diagnosed by a health professional, but to meet the criteria for a diagnosis you must have been feeling persistently down or lost your ability to enjoy your normal pleasures or interests for at least two weeks. In addition, you should have at least two to four of the following symptoms persistently. Tick off how many of the following symptoms of depression you've experienced in the past week.

CHECKLIST OF SYMPTOMS	
Significant weight loss (not because of dieting) or weight gain	
A decrease or increase in appetite	
Difficulty sleeping or sleeping excessively	
Feelings of agitation or irritability	

Tiredness or loss of energy	
Ideas of worthlessness or excessive or inappropriate guilt	
Reduced ability to concentrate or pay attention	
Reduced self-esteem and self-confidence	
A bleak and pessimistic view of the future	
Suicidal thoughts or attempts	

If you are suffering from depression, then your symptoms will be sufficiently distressing to handicap your day-to-day life. Depression is common and about six out of a hundred people have depression. Your lowered mood will vary little from day to day and will not usually change even if your circumstances do. However, it's not unusual for people who have depression to find that their mood is worse in the morning. Individuals' experience of depression varies enormously, especially among adolescents. In some cases, you may feel more anxious or agitated than depressed, or your depression may be masked by irritability, excessive use of alcohol or a preoccupation with your health. Very rarely, people with health anxiety and severe depression may experience delusions of nihilism – for example, they become convinced that their body is rotting, that they are already dead or that they have parasites living under their skin.

Depression nearly always occurs after the onset of health anxiety, suggesting that it is a result of the impact it has on your quality of life. Often, individuals with health anxiety do not have full-blown clinical depression but experience a fluctuating mood, a sense of frustration and irritability. If you suffer from depression or fluctuating mood, then you may also find it helpful to read our book *Manage Your Mood*. After years of preoccupation and social isolation, individuals with health anxiety often experience shame and lack self-compassion which relates to areas other than their health. They think that they are pathetic and should be able to pull themselves together. If shame is a problem, then we would also recommend *The Compassionate Mind Workbook* by Chris Irons and Elaine Beaumont.

Panic disorder

Like a person with health anxiety, someone with panic disorder may experience several worrying physical sensations such as palpitations, feeling short of breath or dizziness. The difference between health anxiety and panic disorder is that the symptoms of panic disorder can be easier to spot. Symptoms occur within ten minutes and are often misinterpreted as evidence of an *immediate* catastrophe – for example, death, suffocation, having a heart attack or going mad now, rather than of a slow lingering illness such as cancer. Health anxiety is like panic disorder in misinterpreting bodily sensations but people with health anxiety also tend to misinterpret other things such as medical information from doctors and the media or test results.

When panic attacks persist, they may lead you to avoid situations or activities where you believe you may have a panic attack – this is called agoraphobia. More information on panic disorder can be found in the book *Overcoming Panic* by Vijaya Manicavasagar and Derrick Silove.

Obsessive compulsive disorder (OCD)

Obsessive compulsive disorder (OCD) is a condition that consists of recurrent intrusive thoughts, images or urges that the person finds distressing or handicapping. These typically include thoughts about contamination, harm (for example, that a gas explosion will occur), aggression or sexual thoughts, and an urge for order or to feel 'just right'. It is associated with avoidance of thoughts and situations that might trigger the obsession or compulsions. Compulsions are actions such as washing or checking, which have to be repeated until the person feels comfortable or certain that nothing bad will happen. Compulsions can also occur in your head, such as repeating a phrase until you feel comfortable. There is often frequent avoidance behaviour in OCD – for example, not wanting to touch anything that is contaminated. About one in one hundred people have OCD.

Health anxiety is thought to be related to OCD. Sometimes the symptoms of OCD and health anxiety overlap, with a grey area between the two. Thus, health anxiety may overlap with fears of contamination (e.g. from AIDS), but in health anxiety there is a greater preoccupation that you have a particular disease or are concerned about contracting it. A separate diagnosis of OCD can be made if there are additional symptoms (e.g. if a person is continuously checking locks or needs order and symmetry). The recommended treatment that has been shown to be effective for OCD is cognitive behavioural therapy (CBT) which is specific for OCD, and SSRI (selective serotonin reuptake inhibitor) antidepressants. Therapy can improve the outcome for most people with OCD. For more details on OCD see our book in this series, *Overcoming Obsessive Compulsive Disorder.*

Body dysmorphic disorder (BDD)

Body dysmorphic disorder (BDD) is a condition that consists of a preoccupation with aspects of your appearance that are neither very noticeable nor seen as abnormal to others. Individuals with BDD usually feel they are ugly, that they are 'not right' and are very self-conscious. They usually have time-consuming rituals such as mirror checking. People with BDD are not vain or narcissistic; they believe themselves to be ugly or defective. They tend to be very secretive and reluctant to seek help because they are afraid that others will think them vain or narcissistic. Some people with BDD will acknowledge that they may be blowing things out of all proportion. At the other extreme, others are so firmly convinced about the nature of their abnormality that they are regarded as having a delusion. Since BDD overlaps with health anxiety, some people believe that not only is a certain feature ugly but that it is a sign of serious disease or allergy.

About two out of one hundred people have BDD. It is recognised to be a hidden disorder since many people with the condition are too ashamed to reveal their main problem.

Both sexes are equally affected by BDD. Typically, the most common concerns are with your skin, followed by concerns about your nose, hair, eyes, chin, lips or the overall body build. People with BDD may complain of a lack of symmetry or feel that something is too big or too small, or that one feature is out of proportion to the rest of the body. Any part of the body may be involved in BDD, including the breasts or genitals.

Although women are more likely to have hair concerns (e.g. that their hair is not symmetrical, that it's the wrong colour, lacks body or there is excessive body hair), men are significantly more concerned with hair thinning or baldness. The sex differences also occur with body size and shape. Women are more likely to be preoccupied with their breasts, hips, weight and legs, usually believing that they are too large or fat. In contrast, men are more likely to be preoccupied with their body build, which has also been described as muscle dysmorphia. Many individuals with BDD have repeatedly sought treatment from dermatologists or cosmetic surgeons, often with little satisfaction, before finally accepting psychological help. The recommended treatments that have been shown to be effective for BDD are cognitive behavioural therapy (CBT) which is specific for BDD, and SSRI antidepressants. For more details on BDD see our book in this series, *Overcoming Body Image Problems including Body Dysmorphic Disorder*.

Generalised anxiety disorder (GAD)

Generalised anxiety disorder (GAD) is a condition character-ised by persistent worry that is difficult to control. However, individuals with GAD often describe themselves as 'being a worrier' all their lives and seek help only when their condition has become severe and uncontrollable. It is very common. For a diagnosis of GAD to be made, the anxiety should occur most of the time and be focused not only on health. For most people with GAD, the content of the worries is most commonly about relationships, health or money, but this often varies and changes over time. People usually experience some of the following feelings most of the time:

- restlessness or feeling keyed up or on edge
- being easily fatigued
- difficulty concentrating or mind going blank
- irritability
- muscle tension (for example, headaches)
- sleep disturbance (difficulty falling or staying asleep, or restless, unsatisfying sleep).

GAD can also cause several physical symptoms and interfere with your ability to function normally. It is a very common problem either alone or in combination with depression or health anxiety. For more information see *Overcoming Worry and Generalised Anxiety Disorder* by Kevin Meares and Mark Freeston in this series.

Alcohol, substance misuse and faddy eating

Sometimes people 'cope' with health anxiety by consuming excessive alcohol or illegal drugs such as street cannabis or stimulants like cocaine. However, the alcohol or drugs then become problems in themselves since street cannabis or stimulants increase paranoia and depressed mood and decrease motivation. To benefit from therapy, individuals will usually need to stop drinking or using substances first, because these will interfere with the therapy. Substances such as cannabis may also be the trigger for the onset of panic and health anxiety.

People with health anxiety (like the rest of us) will find it better to follow a healthy lifestyle. Interestingly, people with health anxiety do not generally follow a healthier lifestyle than the rest of the population – for example, they are just as likely to smoke, drink too much coffee or alcohol, or be inactive. Sometimes health anxiety can lead to extremely unhealthy behaviour either because:

- you are following a very restricted lifestyle or a rigid diet in the belief that it may cure or prevent your medical problem or an allergy, or
- you may be eating a junk diet or neglecting yourself as your mood becomes worse.

We are not saying that a poor diet is *the* cause of your health anxiety or depression, or that if you eat healthily you will not get anxious and depressed in the first place. There are of course many people in the world who follow a poor diet and are not anxious or depressed. Equally, some individuals with anxiety or depression have a healthy diet. But we do say that some people with anxiety or depression may be more sensitive to a poor and chaotic diet and that this is likely to be another factor in keeping them anxious and depressed. A poor diet can aggravate your feeling low, bloated and tired. Giving your brain and body regular and healthy food is an important step you can take to give yourself the best conditions for recovering from anxiety and mood swings. It is also important to avoid substances that will make your mood or anxiety worse or reduce the quality of sleep. There is scientific interest in the use of medical cannabis, but this is very different to street cannabis.

Olfactory reference disorder (ORD)

Olfactory reference disorder (ORD) is a diagnosis used to describe an individual who is preoccupied by body odour, bad breath or the smell of flatulence *not* noticeable to others. This is sometimes regarded as part of health anxiety. It is fortunately uncommon. Such individuals may use perfume to hide the presumed odour. They frequently shower, brush their teeth, change their clothes and ultimately avoid public and social situations where they think their body odour will be noticed. Some people seek frequent reassurance about their body odour. Others have marked avoidance of people and are housebound. Some people with health anxiety are also preoccupied with their body odour, which blends easily with their preoccupation with aspects of their health. For example, if you believe you have a terrible illness, it is not surprising if you also believe that you smell disgusting.

How common is health anxiety?

Health anxiety occurs equally in both men and women. Studies show that about 6 per cent of the population will develop health anxiety in their lifetime, and that between 1 per cent and 5 per cent will have the condition right now. It's estimated that about 10 per cent of people attending their family doctor have a diagnosis of health anxiety. A much larger number consult their doctors with symptoms for which there is no known physical cause.

There is reason to believe that the rate of health anxiety in the population is on the rise. This is because of the many uncertainties and ambiguity in information about COVID. At the time of writing, the world has been dealing with the pandemic of COVID-19 for almost two years. It's not unreasonable to suppose that the extended experience of anxiety about health, with greater pressure to monitor our own health, will have a knock-on effect.

However, there was evidence of increased rates of health anxiety before the pandemic. In recent years, the rates of health anxiety in medical settings show an increase from 15 per cent to 20 per cent. Most of us would guess that one reason for this is the massive amount of health-related information that can be found on the internet. This makes it all too easy for us to diagnose and frighten ourselves with the thought of a serious illness. This has given rise to the term 'cyberchondria'.

When does health anxiety start?

The onset of health anxiety can come at any age, though it commonly starts in adolescence or in young adults. Some people with health anxiety have an excessive worry about a specific illness, which is usually briefer in duration. However, the usual course of health anxiety is to come and go depending on various life stresses. When it returns, it usually affects a different part of your body. Other people with health anxiety have a more long-term, or chronic, form.

The purpose of this book

This book has three main messages:

- Health anxiety is a common problem that causes serious levels of distress; you cannot just snap out of it, and it is nothing to be ashamed of.
- It is not your fault that you have health anxiety. There will be a mix of factors – psychological and biological, as well as social and life experiences – that are pieces in the jigsaw.
- You can overcome your health anxiety if you follow the right plan. This book aims to be your guide to developing your own personalised action plan to overcome your preoccupation and fears related to your health.

We would like to emphasise that those with health anxiety are not alone. It is upsetting and isolating. In serious cases, it can leave an individual unable to function. However, scary and persistent as it is, health anxiety can be overcome.

How following the advice in this book can help

This book can help you learn to apply the principles of a scientifically proven form of psychological therapy called cognitive behavioural therapy (CBT). We have selected the key CBT techniques that have been found to be helpful for health anxiety, and which thousands of people have used to recover. If, for whatever reason, you are unsuccessful, it can be helpful to seek professional help and continue to use this book in conjunction with therapy. If CBT does not work as well as you hoped, adding medication can also help. We explore these options in detail later in the book.

Not all health anxiety is the same

We will cover several different ways in which people experience health anxiety. This book does not contain specific chapters on different presentations of fears of becoming ill. This is a deliberate choice, made because the principles of overcoming health anxiety are essentially the same whatever the focus of your fears. Furthermore, it is not uncommon for health anxiety to change over time and for a 'different' form to become the focus when you have reduced a fear of a particular illness (people often think this will never happen, believing that nothing could be as bad as their current fear). Hence, to get truly lasting freedom from health anxiety, you need to build some general anti-health anxiety attitudes and practices. This often includes having a good tolerance for doubt and resisting your checking.

What is more important is to work on the *processes* that drive your health anxiety, rather than the specific content of your preoccupation with illness.

Some examples of individual experiences with health anxiety

Below are some examples of different experiences of health anxiety. These are not directly taken from the experience of any particular patient we have worked with, but it is striking how similar different individuals' health fears can be. That said, it is not possible to give an illustrative example of every possible presentation, and even similar fears can vary greatly. It's also important to note that, in the same person, the illness they are anxious about can change. The key then is to focus on the *processes* (e.g. difficulty tolerating uncertainty, fear of missing something important, catastrophic thinking, checking, reassurance seeking and avoidance) that are relevant to the maintenance of your own health anxiety. Understanding these processes and how to overcome them is the key to freedom from severe and debilitating anxiety about your health.

Paul's fear of cancer

Following the death of his father two years earlier, Paul, aged sixty-six, became preoccupied with the idea that he would develop bowel cancer. He had known one of his father's friends to have multiple sclerosis and had become particularly afraid of the way it seemed to come and go without warning, leaving more permanent damage behind each time. Paul spent at least five hours a day preoccupied with his health. He had become acutely tuned in to his body for any possible signs of disease. He was especially anxious about any feelings of discomfort in his stomach, but he would often worry about other physical sensations too, fearing they could be 'secondary' tumours. At times he would be afraid that he might develop cancer, and in his more acutely anxious moments he'd become convinced he had the disease. Paul would check his stools when he went to the toilet for any sign of blood or mucus and would frequently feel unsure that what he was looking at was normal. He bought several 'home detection kits' for self-testing for bowel cancer, and would sometimes feel reassured for a short while, but often wondered how reliable the tests really were. He would spend hours each day on the internet looking for symptoms of bowel cancer, looking for reassurance that he did not have his most feared illness. He would also research health foods and ways of avoiding environmental toxins in the hope that he could reduce his risk of serious illness.

A doctor had told Paul that his symptoms were caused by anxiety, but he remained anxious because he couldn't find the 100 per cent certainty he craved that he was not ill or going to become ill. He would use books and the internet to check lists of symptoms if he did ever feel any physical sensations he was unsure of. He would make frequent trips to see his doctor, taking with him notes he'd made of the time, bodily location, intensity and duration of his physical sensations. He never felt reassured for very long and would often ask his doctor for more tests and screening, but also would worry that he could have a form of cancer that wasn't readily picked up on tests. Paul knew that he was 'a bit of a hypochondriac' and started to worry that he would have a 'cry wolf' problem, in that he'd had so many 'false alarms' that his doctor wouldn't take him seriously if he really were ill. He decided that he would have to give his doctor as much information as possible and to insist on another referral to a specialist to prevent this from happening. However, he could see his doctor becoming stressed when he saw him, and it occurred to him that perhaps his doctor knew he was ill and was too afraid to tell him.

Paul's wife worked as a schoolteacher and had come to dread checking her telephone messages at break times because there would inevitably be a message from Paul desperate to speak to her for reassurance. In the evenings Paul began to drink excessive amounts of alcohol to reduce his anxiety, but this put further strain on his marriage.

Adrian's fear of having a heart attack

Adrian was forty-five. Most of his life he had been a worrier, but this had not been a major problem. He had become increasingly worried about his heart after he felt that it was missing beats. He'd had several consultations with his doctor, who had reassured him that there was no evidence of a heart problem. Adrian checked his pulse and blood pressure daily. To try to put his mind at rest his doctor sent him to see a specialist heart doctor. Adrian's reaction to this referral was that he thought 'My doctor must be more concerned than he's saying, otherwise he wouldn't have sent me for a test'. This meant that his anxiety became much worse the following week, and eventually he paid to see a private heart specialist, who carried out some 24-hour ECG testing and reported back that he could lose a bit of weight, but that his test results were within normal limits. After the appointment, it occurred to Adrian that he might not have given the cardiologist all the information he needed. What if he did not have a big enough missed beat on the day of the test? He spent hours trying to think of better ways of describing his symptoms, becoming ever more preoccupied and distressed. He would switch between this and trying to reassure himself by telling himself to be more rational and to pull himself together. This led to more doubts and checking on the internet. He became an expert on his own heart rhythm and became convinced that his heart was fragile and more prone than average to problems. This led him to avoid taking strenuous exercise, and the concern then nagged at the back of his mind that he might be increasing his risk of heart disease by not being fit enough.

Anne's fear of breast cancer

Anne was fifty-three and worried that she might develop breast cancer. A few years earlier she had a benign lump removed and hadn't really worried until her son won an award at school. Her life seemed to be going very well and she was in general feeling very happy. However, it crossed her mind 'wouldn't it be awful if something came along to spoil all this'. In the next image that entered her mind she was in a hospital bed, her child and her husband both looking deeply concerned. Anne was somewhat superstitious and saw the image as a portent for the future. She thought it was a warning that she had become too complacent about her breasts and so she started checking them for lumps each day. She noticed that they were more tender, so became increasingly concerned, seeking multiple consultations with several doctors. Frequently searching the internet, she was convinced that it was entirely reasonable to look for certainty about something as important as her health. She believed that none of the doctors she saw took a detailed enough interest in her concerns, thus becoming increasingly worried that something might have been missed.

Ibrahim's fear of going mad

Ibrahim was preoccupied by a fear that he would go mad. He had an unhappy childhood, since his father was an alcoholic and the family had lived in fear of his rages. Ibrahim was terrified that he would lose control of his mind, develop schizophrenia, fail to respond to treatment, end up in a locked psychiatric ward, and lose his job, wife, house and children. He had a mental image of looking through the narrow window of a hospital ward and watching his wife and children visit. They looked sad, since they were coming to terms with the fact that he was irretrievably lost to mental illness. He therefore checked his thoughts for any sign of madness or signs of unreality. One of his main anxiety symptoms was of his surroundings feeling unreal, a sensation that he tried desperately to fight off. He frequently reassured himself and thought about what he was experiencing. He would avoid walking past an old asylum that was on his normal route to work. He avoided reading any references in the media to madness.

Ali's fear of motor neurone disease

Ali became preoccupied and anxious that he might have early signs of motor neurone disease (MND) after noticing a twitch on his arm on a few occasions. Although he knew that the twitch usually followed a heavy training session at the gym, Ali began to use the internet to research other possible explanations. This substantially increased his fears that the twitching could be the early signs of something serious. Ali had in fact long had a degree of fear of degenerative neurological diseases and had found the condition 'locked-in syndrome' very distressing to imagine when reading about it a couple of years earlier (a condition in which the patient is conscious and aware of their surroundings but unable to move or communicate). Reading up extensively on the internet about early signs of the condition and joining MND forums to learn more fuelled his belief that he had MND. Ali had been seen by a neurologist;

a doctor had referred him, hoping it would provide some lasting relief. The neurologist carried out a 'nerve conductivity test', showing all was well, and briefly reassured Ali that the twitches were 'benign fasciculations', but Ali quickly returned to his conviction that he had MND. Most mornings involved spending several minutes watching his arms and legs for signs of twitching and 'tuning in' to bodily sensations during the day. He very carefully avoided any news articles, TV programmes or films about neurological problems in case they might trigger anxiety and make it hard to focus at work or at home.

Mariam's fear of skin cancer

Since she had a cancerous mole removed a couple of years previously, Mariam worried about skin cancer; not only for herself, but for her husband and children too. She would regularly check her skin and that of her children. Her husband refused to let her check his body, so she would try and look at his skin when he wasn't aware. She also sought reassurance from him and he would often become irritated by this. She insisted that her children had annual 'mole-mapping' and had several further moles removed in case they might become cancerous. She was very reluctant to expose her skin to the sun and often lectured her family on the importance of avoiding excessive exposure to sunlight. Her grandfather had died of skin cancer when she was a little girl and this had left her with a sense that the condition was inevitable, and she must do all she could to delay it harming her or her loved ones. She would check the internet regularly for any advances in the detection and treatment.

Lian's fear of dementia

Lian had a fear mainly that she might get an early onset form of Alzheimer's disease, but she worried about other forms of brain disease, such as having a brain tumour. She would monitor her mind and try and test her memory in a variety of ways, such as testing her recall of things she read and filling out tests on the internet. Several times a week she would research brain health on the internet. She was extremely well informed of the symptoms of numerous brain diseases and the latest advice on how to prevent them. She was often plagued with the image of attending an appointment with her doctor and being told she had an incurable disease that might have been prevented if only she had detected it earlier. Consequently, she hardly ever visited the doctor and avoided hospitals or medical dramas as much as possible.

Victoria's preoccupation with a fear of blood-borne illness

Victoria was afraid that she would contract some form of disease that would be carried in her blood. Initially she worried about hepatitis and AIDS, but as she investigated further on the internet, the scope of possible illnesses she worried about grew. She worried that she might have a disease but be unaware of it, and that she would one day discover this disease and look back over her life with fear and regret. She was afraid she would not be treated with dignity or properly communicated with. She hated when doctors did not give her proper feedback. This was a lifelong tendency to health anxiety that generally worsened when she was stressed for other reasons. When she was much younger, the sudden death of her grandmother and an aunt she was close to was relevant, as she never understood the circumstances of their deaths.

We'll return to some of our characters later in the book.

Famous figures with health anxiety

If you have health anxiety, then you are not alone. Some of the figures throughout history who have been reported as having health anxiety include:

- Charles Darwin (preoccupied with fatigue and gut problems)
- Alfred Lord Tennyson (preoccupied with fear that his eyesight might fail)
- Emmanuel Kant (preoccupied with his breathing and headaches)
- Adolf Hitler (became convinced that he had throat cancer)

Treatments for health anxiety

Until relatively recently, health anxiety was regarded as a chronic disorder that was distressing to both patient and doctor. It was regarded as being difficult to treat, because medicine had little to offer other than reassurance. This has now changed, and the good news is that health anxiety is a highly treatable problem. This book outlines some of the principles of cognitive behavioural therapy that are used in overcoming health anxiety, and we hope that it will help you work toward making a full recovery.

It's true that health anxiety can be tough to overcome and can call for a lot of hard work, but this is far from impossible for most people. As we'll show, a good amount of recovery in fact comes from working considerably less hard and from stopping your current coping strategies. What's more, getting on with other rewarding, productive and enjoyable aspects of your life is an integral part of recovery and will help drive health anxiety out of your life.

Cognitive behavioural therapy (CBT)

The principles in this book come from an approach to psychological treatment called cognitive behavioural therapy (CBT). CBT is the most extensively researched and proven psychological treatment for health anxiety and numerous other emotional problems. Below is a brief description of the approach of CBT specific for health anxiety.

Cognitive change refers to developing an alternative understanding of the problem. This might involve changing the *meaning* you give to your bodily sensations or images. The more extreme or catastrophic the meaning we give something, the more extreme and negative the emotion we feel. Because our brains have a 'better safe than sorry' bias, humans easily misinterpret things and give them a more threatening meaning than they deserve. In the case of health anxiety, the heart of the problem is the way *normal* bodily sensations and images are *interpreted* as abnormal or as a sign of illness, and this has to be resolved. In health anxiety, there is commonly an intolerance of uncertainty. This is the distress from 'not knowing' whether you might have a serious illness. Health anxiety can be related to a sense of increased vulnerability to illness or disease, which can drive excessive checking, self-monitoring and fear. This can sometimes be related to your experiences as a younger person; either being overexposed to, or being overprotected from, illness and/or death.

Recovery from health anxiety involves developing a more realistic and helpful way of understanding the bodily sensations that you worry about so much. Unfortunately, other emotions associated with health anxiety, such as depression and shame, tend to make your worrying even more powerful. The key is to 'detach', to distance yourself from your catastrophic thoughts and to tolerate not knowing for certain. Remember, your brain is trying to keep you safe and will send you lots of warning signals: sometimes we all need to learn when *not* to listen to warnings. Think of a car with a faulty alarm which goes off every time the wind changes. If we know about the fault, we interpret the significance of the alarm differently.

Your 'anti-health anxiety' aim should be to truly accept bodily sensations or movements (for example, a tremor) and images without engaging in any mental activity or behaviour that makes you think you can prevent the disease or reduce your uncertainty. Behaviour change in CBT refers to changing the way you *respond* to your bodily sensations and the thoughts or images your mind produces about them. Remember that what you do in your mind, such as mental checking or deliberately recalling a conversation with a doctor, is a form of behaviour or 'doing' something.

We understand that changing your behaviour is tough and requires courage. You will come across the term 'Exposure and Response Prevention' (ERP), which involves you making a deliberate choice, for therapeutic reasons, to confront your fears and resist any compulsion or safety-seeking behaviour in the face of that fear.

Another term we will use is a 'behavioural experiment'. These look very similar to exposure because they involve doing something uncomfortable. However, they are designed to test a particular prediction or expectation; to gather data and see how things work. Some thoughts are not directly testable (and this is *not* a block in recovery): a classic example is whether you might have a variant of your feared illness that is not detectable using current medical tests. Instead, you can run experiments to test whether your findings best fit your fear or belief, or best fit the idea that you have a problem of worrying about your health and find it difficult to tolerate *not knowing, not being in control, or that you might miss something important to solve.* What matters is that you learn to tolerate the feelings of anxiety ('exposure and response prevention') *and* test your expectations on how the processes that maintain your anxiety work ('behavioural experiments'). In this book, we have used the term 'exposure' as a shorthand to cover both these elements.

Effective CBT for health anxiety usually contains the following components, although it may not be necessary to use all of them:

- Understanding the link between physical sensations, thinking, attention, emotion and behavioural components of your own health anxiety.
- Testing out your fears and resisting doing the things you do to try and feel more reassured (e.g. checking, researching information on the internet, reassurance-seeking, seeking medical investigations).
- Practising allowing catastrophic thoughts and images about illness or dying without responding or 'engaging' (trying to get rid of them, planning, examining, reassuring yourself, etc.).
- Cutting back or stopping 'monitoring' your health. This often involves deliberately re-focusing your attention away from your body and on to the environment around you.
- Becoming aware of unhelpful thoughts and attitudes you have towards illness or death.
- Learning to tolerate uncertainty and reduce excessive responsibility. This can help with reducing your excessive fear of missing an important symptom.
- Learning to spot yourself engaging in worrying about your health and to 'switch' the focus of your attention

to bring your mind back into dealing with real life in the here-and-now.

- Putting time and energy back into things that are important to you so you can improve the quality of your life and reduce the amount of time you spend thinking about your health.
- Developing a balanced plan for taking appropriate care of your health.
- Dealing effectively with the fact that you will one day die, without excessively worrying about it.

Looking at the list above, what do you imagine are likely to be the most important steps for you to take to overcome your health anxiety?

_____

_____

_____

_____

_____

Medication for health anxiety

Medication (usually a form of antidepressant called a selective serotonin reuptake inhibitor – 'SSRI') is not usually recommended for mild to moderate symptoms of health anxiety. However, if your doctor believes that the health anxiety symptoms are likely to get worse (or if the symptoms have lasted for a long time), medication may still be recommended. Antidepressant medication is more commonly recommended as an option in treating more severe symptoms of health anxiety, especially when depression is present. However, it can also be helpful in moderate to severe health anxiety in the absence of depression. We discuss the use of medication in more detail in Chapter 12.

Combining medication with CBT

In general, we do not recommend using medication as the only remedy for health anxiety because it may be less effective and there is usually a higher rate of relapse when a person stops taking the medication. That said, we need a lot more research into health anxiety.

Medication is more often used in severe health anxiety. For people with severe health anxiety, results are probably better when the medication is combined with CBT (and most people need to take medication for at least a year, which may be beyond the course of therapy). This said, given that there are many different types of health anxiety, some people may do fine on medication alone and get back to a normal life with just that. Whatever approach you take, make sure you monitor your progress using the rating scales in this book so you can decide (with your therapist or doctor) what is helping and whether to try something else.

2

Getting the most out of using this book

At the end of the last chapter, we introduced you to some of the main principles of cognitive behavioural therapy for health anxiety. This chapter aims to add a little more depth to some of those ideas. We'll also offer some suggestions on working through this in ways that we hope will make it as helpful to you as possible. At the end, we'll cover some of the more common reservations that we've learned people have about using a self-help book and offer some responses.

Some clarifications

We have noticed over the years that, in trying to help people think differently, therapists sometimes use terms that cause some confusion. We will quickly define some key words to help clear up some of that confusion.

Acceptance of a bodily sensation, or acceptance of the thought of the possibility of illness, does not mean that:

- We are saying it doesn't matter.

- You are resigning yourself to suffering from an illness or to an early death.

- You should just give up any attempts to look after your health.

Acceptance means willingness to be open to an experience as it is. It may mean learning to cope with uncertainty, the possibility of an illness, or living life as fully as you can even if you are or become ill.

Carrying out an experiment and testing out a thought does not mean you should try to get a definitive answer as to whether you have your feared illness. The main emphasis in testing out your predictions is on *how your health anxiety works* (e.g. whether checking makes you more or less unsure). Most importantly, it means seeing what happens if you treat your health anxiety 'as if' you are wholly confident that your problem is one of anxiety or worry.

Tolerate the discomfort does not mean that:

- We think your emotional distress is insignificant, mild or unimportant.

- We think this is easy.

It means being prepared to experience your anxiety and not escape by using a strategy like seeking or checking for reassurance to alleviate your discomfort. This takes courage. It means 'feeling the fear' yet choosing not to escape from the fear or avoid it.

Try to work through the chapters in the book with an open mind.

No matter how severe your health anxiety, how long you've had the problem, or how many times you have tackled it before, there's every chance you can make significant gains by following the principles outlined in this book. It's understandable that with a problem that can be as consuming and distressing as health anxiety, people doubt their ability to overcome it without specialist help. However, CBT is much like physiotherapy or training for sport or fitness. Ultimately, while we need some guidance on what to do, it's regular training and practice that have the biggest impact.

There's also now a lot of self-help books on the market and it is very difficult to know which will be most helpful.

We've done our best to inform the content of this book with up-to-date research, as well as our combined sixty-plus years of experience in delivering treatment. So, whether this is the very first time you've thought about trying to break free from severe and persistent anxiety about your health, or you've tried many times before, take a fresh look at your health anxiety, clarify how your problem works, and build a deliberate plan to overcome it using the steps in this book.

Keeping records of your progress

To help stay motivated, it is beneficial to have a history of what you have done so far and a measure of change. Humans tend to concentrate on what is not going well rather than what is, so keeping records provides a helpful reminder of the work you've put in and the changes that have resulted. Checking the severity of your health anxiety on the questionnaires at regular intervals (we suggest at least once a fortnight) will help to give you a feel for how things are changing. Here you can use a buddy or an alarm to remind you when to repeat the measures.

Consider finding an ally

Overcoming health anxiety can be tough, so it can be well worth enlisting some support from someone willing to help you follow the ideas outlined in this book. In CBT, such a supporter is often called a 'co-therapist'. This person might be a friend, partner or relative. Allies can be of enormous value and support you in numerous ways, for example:

- Helping you increase your commitment to your exposure tasks.
- Helping you to review your progress. This might include feedback on how exposure and behavioural experiments are going, sharing frequency records and ratings of progress.
- Sharing with you their examples of unexplained bodily sensations, catastrophic thoughts about such bodily sensations, images and doubts.
- Accompanying you on an exposure exercise (e.g. watching a film about your feared illness or visiting a hospital).
- Helping to come up with imaginative ideas for exposure and response prevention tasks.
- Helping to troubleshoot stuck points.
- Helping you to discover or rediscover activities that help keep your mind focused on the outside world and the here and now.
- Giving general support and encouragement – probably the most essential part!

If you have an ally it can help for them to work through this book with you.

The person will need to be prepared to act as your co-therapist: to read through this book and set aside sufficient time, reliably, to sit down with you (e.g. for about half an hour a couple of times a week at the start). You should emphasise that they are there to act as a supporter in *your* plan to overcome *your* health anxiety. Hopefully, they'll have creative suggestions and ideas, but it's critical that you negotiate a plan before you begin to implement it. It is also worth deciding beforehand what you would prefer your ally to do or say should you become over-anxious, stressed or angry. We cover this more in Chapter 11, which is written for friends and family.

Later in the book, we will walk you through how to identify support and how to seek informal and professional help. In this section we will help you evaluate the various treatments and medications available. Finally, we will help you consider how to maintain the gains you have made in order to reduce the chances of relapse.

Being optimistic about recovery

Have you ever read, or been told to your face, that health anxiety is a chronic problem you just have to learn to live with? Such comments are common and deeply unhelpful. They are apt to diminish any hope of freedom from the tyranny of health anxiety. Let's set the record straight: health anxiety can take a chronic course if left untreated. However, with the correct specific approach, people *can and do* overcome their health anxiety. This is true even if they have had the problem for a very long time and even if it is severe: refuse to participate with your health anxiety and it will wither and die.

Understand that you are not alone

It's estimated that as many as 6 per cent of the population will develop health anxiety in their lifetime, so you're very definitely not alone. We are bombarded with health-related information and unprecedented pressure to take personal responsibility for our health. With changing advice on how to look after our health and encouragement to 'spot problems early', many worry about their health. Unlimited access to health-related information on the internet has further increased our tendency to 'self-diagnose'. Further, researchers estimate that as many as half of us will experience a psychological problem at some point in our lives. Many of these problems will involve emotions that are common in health anxiety such as anxiety, shame and depression, and share common processes like overthinking, avoidance and safety-seeking behaviours.

Think of improving your mental health like improving your physical fitness

If you want to get fit, you will know that carrying the odd bag of shopping or running for the bus will not be sufficient. Improved fitness and flexibility come from a commitment to regular training and activity. It can be helpful to bear this in mind when considering the deliberate planned exposure and experiments. These will be at the heart of your recovery. While you can certainly practise these techniques whenever your health anxiety is activated, such occasions tend to occur inconsistently and often at inconvenient times. The key to becoming mentally fitter, and therefore better equipped to overcome your health anxiety, is deliberate training and rehabilitation. Think about the daily exercises you might need to do if you were seeing a physiotherapist for a back or knee problem. Consider the amount of exercise – walks, runs, swims, sessions at the gym – you might do if you needed to make significant improvements to your health. Imagine the care and dedication that you might need to put in if you were recovering from a serious physical health problem. Overcoming health anxiety really is no different. Exposure tasks are planned activities – they are not just things you respond to when you are triggered.

Focus upon the benefits of breaking free from health anxiety both to yourself and the people close to you

In psychotherapy and self-help there is a popular idea that true change will only come about when you want to change for yourself. However, we humans are social animals – we've evolved to be part of a group. It's entirely natural to be motivated to change because you want to improve the lives of others. If you feel motivated to improve your health anxiety because you want to be a better partner or parent, or you want your parents to worry less about you, this does not invalidate your actions and you will still benefit. Always remember, tackling your health anxiety will reduce your suffering.

Most people with health anxiety find that they begin to prioritise their compulsions over other interests, people and activities, losing vast quantities of time and energy. This then has a knock-on effect on other aspects of life. Perhaps you find yourself late for activities and appointments or avoiding places or situations. This might be the result of an effort to reduce stress and anxiety or feeling compelled to give in to compulsions. You may be missing out on social activities or relationships, or may avoid taking on more challenging jobs due to your fears. You might spend vast amounts of time checking the Internet. Significant others are often directly affected by becoming involved in compulsions and reassurance or are indirectly affected by worrying about you and the restrictions the condition is placing on your life and sometimes on theirs too. Consider how different your life might be if you did not have health anxiety: the way you would feel and the amount of time and energy you would have for people and activities that truly engage you and make you happy.

Ask '*how am I keeping my health anxiety going?*' more than '*what can be done to make my health anxiety go away?*'

If you're deeply troubled by intrusive sensations or images, then it's extremely likely that you are hoping to avoid those experiences in some way. The bedrock of your recovery will be a good list of the mental and physical strategies you use to avoid or escape from your worries. You need to define these so that you can break away from them.

Be willing to experience discomfort

Terms like 'no pain, no gain' are common in gyms and exercise classes and we all know that change involves 'stepping out of your comfort zone'. It's most important to distinguish between reducing short-term discomfort using a compulsion and taking steps to improve your health anxiety in the long term. This is because short-term solutions tend to maintain your suffering in the long run. We all find change uncomfortable and overcoming health anxiety involves a kind of double discomfort: facing your fears *and* developing new habits. The art is to try to make the emotional discomfort of fighting your health anxiety as productive as possible by really committing to change and being as consistent as you can.

Make the most of metaphors and helpful images

As the saying goes, a picture paints a thousand words and there is growing evidence from research on the value of images therapy. Many people find developing a metaphor for their health anxiety, or a visual image of it or the process of breaking free from it, to be helpful. Here are a few examples:

Health anxiety as a bully

Thinking of your health anxiety as a bully is a metaphor that very many people find helps them to separate themselves from their health anxiety and be more objective. It's a great image for the tyrannical nature of health anxiety: particularly the evil sort of bully that pretends to be your friend, while consistently working against you. It pretends that it is keeping you or others safe, which is surely a good thing? Like any effective bully, it thrives on persuading you to give in to it to avoid its threats. It is trying to help you stay more in control of your thoughts so that you won't feel worse in the future. And all it asks is that you carry out a bit of a compulsion or use some avoidance – so you can feel better. Lies, lies, lies and you can bet he or she will be back tomorrow. Or later today. Or in a few minutes. Luckily, we all know the best way to deal with bullies – refuse to engage with their demands. Like all bullies, the health anxiety bully is insecure and frightened. Bullies cope by being aggressive and forcing you to submit to their insecurities to feel in control. Try to talk to your health anxiety bully to understand his or her motivation and fears. State clearly that you understand their fears, but they are not acting in your best interests. Try to make clear boundaries about what you are not prepared to do as you both want a long-term solution.

An alternative to the bully – your overprotective brain

We do understand that viewing your health anxiety as a bully isn't for everyone. The reality is that your brain is probably trying too hard to protect you or others. In this sense it can be more helpful to think of health anxiety as being a bit more like an overprotective parent, guardian or grandparent. But at the point of having to resist their long-established, almost automatic, almost impossible to resist, often frightening to resist, compulsion, many people have told us they found thinking of it as like standing up to a bully rather helpful.

The unwelcome party guest

The unwelcome party guest is a metaphor used to illustrate a common human problem when someone is avoiding difficult thoughts and feelings. This is a story about a person who decides one day to throw a party and has an unwelcome guest arrive in the form of his unpleasant neighbour. Think of a name for your own gatecrasher to use as a representation of your intrusive thoughts, images, doubts or sensations and the emotional discomfort that comes with him – he is rude, badly behaved and smells from poor personal hygiene. The point of the metaphor is that the person throwing the party (us) tries to deal with the unwelcome guest by throwing him out. The gatecrasher comes back. We throw him out again and then stand by the door to keep him out. But then we can't enjoy the party or look after our guests (trying too hard to control our mind and emotions removes time and effort from what we find important in the way we want to engage with the world around us). Our party host has a realisation. He lets his neighbour in and just gets on with the party. Sure, he'd rather he wasn't there, but letting him just get on with it is a whole heap better than being engaged with trying to get rid of him. What is the best way of making sure the neighbour doesn't spoil the party next time? Send him an invitation, just as you are doing with your deliberate exposure and response prevention. Many people find this is an especially compelling way of thinking about their intrusive sensations and feelings and the best way of handling them.

Your health anxiety-free twin – a metaphor for setting goals and/or planning for alternative behaviour

Imagine you have a twin, the same as you in every respect except for the fact that she is wholly free from health anxiety. Asking yourself what she would do can be an incredibly helpful short cut to identifying a healthier way to behave.

Be patient, persevere and normalise setbacks on the road to recovery

Overcoming health anxiety is rarely a smooth, linear process; it's a journey of ups and downs, like learning a new skill – driving, a musical instrument, walking again after an injury. Overcoming health anxiety is different of course, but growth, learning and rehabilitation are almost always accompanied by frustrations, setbacks and moments when we think to ourselves '*I'll never be able to do this!*' Yes, overcoming health anxiety can be challenging: you are human, with all the strengths and weaknesses that implies. Breaking free from health anxiety may differ from other challenges, but not as much as you might think, or others might suggest. Recall other times you've overcome adversity or changed or mastered a skill to help you find the inspiration you need for that extra push. And above all, don't give up!

If at first you don't succeed, try, try again

A significant number of the people we see have had several previous attempts at treatment for their health anxiety and have had the problem for many years. In many ways this is not at all surprising. Achieving something so life-changing is a challenge. On average it takes someone seven attempts to give up smoking. Seven. Nicotine is addictive and smoking is associated with compelling triggers, so giving up is hard.

If you've tried and failed to overcome your health anxiety before, take a few moments to consider whether you properly attacked the problem. Did you put enough effort into stopping your checking, self-monitoring, internet-searching or attempts to gain reassurance? Did you practise enough deliberate exposure? Think about what you could have done differently and what, through failing, you have learned about the nature of your health anxiety. You can use this to build a better plan for recovery. You are the key person who can improve your mental health.

Some common fears about using a book to help overcome your problems

Below we discuss four common reservations about using a self-help book for overcoming health anxiety and we hope to lay any fears to rest.

1. 'Thinking about the problem will make it worse.'

The opposite is true. When individuals try to avoid thinking about the processes in their health anxiety and what they can do about it, their problems persist and over time become more difficult to solve. In this book we aim to try to help you develop a good psychological understanding of what is keeping your problem going and therefore what you can do to put an end to severe and persistent worries about your health.

2. 'I've heard that CBT is about testing your beliefs and finding out that they aren't realistic. My fears are based on something "real" i.e. it's a fact that I will get ill and will eventually die, so a psychological approach won't reduce my fear.'

A fundamental principle in CBT is that the type and intensity of emotion we experience are greatly influenced by the meaning we attach to things. It may not be possible, or even wise, to totally remove all anxiety about illness or death, but if you could reduce your fear to some extent, would you? To do this you might find a new, less extreme and more helpful outlook. To strengthen and maintain this perspective,

47

you'll need to act and focus your attention in ways that support it.

3. 'I feel so ashamed of having health anxiety and it is my fault, so I cannot expect help.'

This is very important: it's not your fault that you have health anxiety. The exact cause of health anxiety is not known. What we do know is that being human means that you are born with a tricky brain. It is constantly juggling between keeping you safe, keeping you rational and acting in your best interests. You will also have inherited genes, from parents you did not choose, and you will have had various experiences that have shaped you throughout your life.

It is not your fault that you have health anxiety, but it *is* your responsibility to overcome it as no-one else can do this for you.

4. 'The physical sensations I experience are very real – it's not "all in my head" so surely I cannot (and should not) learn to ignore them.'

There is no doubt that the bodily sensations (or sometimes movements) that you experience are very real. It's possible that some of those sensations are caused by anxiety itself and it may be that the amount of 'signal' your brain detects from certain sensations is increased because of the way you are focusing your attention on your body (remember, we include your mind and brain in 'body'). Our brain naturally filters out and ignores a very great deal of signal from our body, and it might be that you are accidentally interfering with this process. The main question is this: how helpful has it been to you to be preoccupied and anxious about illness to the extent that you have been? The aim is for you to be able to regain control of how much time, attention and energy you give to your health and of the way you care for your health.

What if CBT doesn't work for me?

If you are unsuccessful, then don't give up: you can always seek further help in a more specialist setting and use this book alongside it. At least three-quarters of people with health anxiety can make substantial improvements through a formal course of CBT. It's important to note, however, that 'professional help' doesn't mean that you get to 'hand your brain over to medical science' for someone else to fix. Very often the more accomplished the therapist, the better they will be at helping 'your brain to take the strain'. Only you can break your own mental and behavioural habits, so please don't fall into the trap of waiting to get professional help on the basis that it might be an easier option. It is very likely not to be.

Make a note here of any key doubts or reservations you have about working on your health anxiety, with a response to each that will help encourage you to really throw yourself into the process. To help with this, try to imagine you were coaching a loved one or good friend.

_____

_____

_____

_____

_____

_____

_____

3

Defining your problem, setting goals and measuring progress

Overcoming health anxiety is like any problem solving; a good solution depends on a well-defined problem, and it's often easier to solve a problem if you break it down a bit. This chapter aims to help you identify some of the key parts that make up your health anxiety, so that you understand your problem a bit better and can start to identify specific targets for change.

Feelings and emotions

Experiencing health anxiety often brings a mixture of different emotions. Typically, the main experience is (of course) fear and *anxiety*. However, *depression*, disgust, anger and shame are also common emotions felt by people with this problem. With health anxiety, the problem is not that you are just anxious, but that your anxiety is particularly severe and persistent.

Anxiety can produce a variety of physical sensations too, including feeling hot and sweaty, having a racing heart, feeling faint, wobbly or shaky, experiencing muscle tension (for example, headaches), having stomach upsets or diarrhoea, to list a few. These, too, may be further misinterpreted so that a vicious circle ensues.

If, however, you are becoming despondent and hopeless about the future, you may feel down or emotionally 'numb', feeling that life has lost its fun. These are core symptoms of depression. In addition, you might start to experience sleep problems, lose your appetite and sexual interests. You might be brooding about the past, feel more irritable and have difficulty concentrating. With depression, people can react by becoming withdrawn and inactive and wanting to avoid situations or activities that are painful.

In addition, depression can fuel worries about your health. Indeed, in certain cultures and amongst the elderly, complaints about body sensations can be the primary symptoms reported when the person suffers from depression. Common body sensations and changes that occur in depression include:

- feeling fatigued
- sleep disturbance
- changes in sex drive
- changes in appetite
- headaches
- constipation
- aches and pains

So, if your mood has been low in addition to your feeling anxious it might be very helpful to consider depression as a possible cause of physical or mental sensations. Depression also makes our minds much more likely to generate negative thoughts and images. The other critical effect that depression can have is to make a person become far more receptive to negative information. Thus, if a negative thought or image (e.g. an image of yourself ill or of your funeral) crosses your mind, low mood may be one of the reasons. Again, it is worth considering this as an alternative to believing that the image must be important or a sign that the picture in your mind will come true. People with health anxiety and severe depression should seek help immediately if they feel suicidal or have strange beliefs (e.g. that their body is rotting or that they have cancer, when they don't). Sometimes people believe that they would be better off dead so that their relatives do not have to cope with their suffering from a feared illness like cancer.

Can you identify the dominant emotions about your health (e.g. anxiety, fear, depression, shame, guilt, disgust or anger)?

_____

_____

_____

Physical sensations and other bodily experiences

The physical sensations and other bodily experiences (such as a mark on your skin) are very real. Only you can tell people what you experience, so don't let anyone tell you the sensations are imagined or all in your head. But some sensations (like dizziness or tiredness) that are part of 'normal' heath may be misinterpreted as evidence of a severe illness. Thus, a headache caused by muscle tension may be interpreted as a brain tumour. A blemish on your skin may be misinterpreted as cancer. Feelings of unreality may be interpreted as a sign of schizophrenia. Other people might have a long-term illness such as epilepsy or diabetes and have symptoms related to their illness but again misinterpret their significance. Such symptoms can be constant over time or change and vary in intensity.

Can you identify your physical sensations that you currently worry about, check or seek reassurance about?

_____

_____

_____

Intrusive images

Intrusive images refer to pictures or felt impressions that just pop into your mind, especially when you are more anxious about your health. Images are not just pictures in your mind but can also be felt sensations.

Pictures are said to convey a thousand words and often reflect your mood. If you are very anxious, you might have mental pictures of going mad or dying. People often experience such images from an observer perspective, that is looking back at yourself and believing that the picture in your mind is a predictor of the future. For example, a woman with health anxiety had an image of herself dead with her soul floating in space. This was frightening for her as she felt she would still be having thoughts and feelings but would not be in control of the situation around her.

Images usually feel as if they are true or accurate and relevant now. This, however, is questionable, since such pictures may be linked to bad experiences and are like ghosts from the past, which have not been updated. So, if you have had a bad experience of an illness in the family or of a doctor who had missed a diagnosis then that memory can become stuck in time and influence the present. To treat images as if they were reality can create many problems; to change that involves recognising that you are experiencing only a picture in your mind, not current reality.

Can you identify any images that you experience when you are anxious about your health?

Thoughts

As well as images, you may have thoughts and doubts about yourself becoming, for example, seriously ill or going mad. Alternatively, you may believe that you are already ill and dying. The threat to your health might be partly realistic (e.g. you have diabetes) and may be from the past (e.g. a memory) or what you think could happen in the future. When anxiety dominates the picture, you may be overestimating the degree of danger to yourself or others. This is closely linked to the sensations and any images you have identified; for example, a tremor is misinterpreted as evidence of a severe neurological condition. Your mind tends to think of all the possible bad things that could occur. This is called 'catastrophising' and is a natural part of your mind's 'threat system'.

As we discuss below, your mind will want to know for certain or have a guarantee that you will not die or suffer from a severe illness. This leads to worrying about how to solve non-existent problems and to control as many of your bodily functions as you can or to plan to deal with all the possible problems that do not arise. One of the problems is that your thoughts become fused with past experiences and accepted as facts in the 'here and now'. Therefore, you develop a pattern of thinking that is like holding a prejudice against information that does not fit with your fears.

It's hugely important to recognise that thoughts about your physical sensations or health are just that – thoughts, not reality. Learning to normalise and accept these negative thoughts and images willingly as 'just thoughts' and not buying into them is an important part of overcoming health anxiety.

Can you identify any thoughts that you experience when you are anxious about your health?

_____

_____

_____

Worry

You might cope with health anxiety by trying to control your thoughts or by suppressing them, which can mean the thoughts enter your mind more frequently. You may be worrying a great deal, which means trying to solve potential problems in the future. This usually takes the form of trying to answer or solve 'what if . . . ?' questions. Examples include 'What if I get cancer?' followed by 'I can get a test done now', but this triggers the thought 'What if the test is not accurate and I die. How will my children cope when I have died?' To overcome the problem, the main thing is to try and avoid engaging with answering such thoughts (as they just create more questions) and build up your tolerance of uncertainty.

Can you identify any worries or 'What if . . . ' questions that you are trying to solve about your health?

_____

_____

_____

Brooding

You may be trying to 'put right' or make sense of past events by brooding on them, perhaps mulling over them constantly. It is also called 'ruminating' or 'overthinking'. You are probably trying to solve problems that cannot be solved or analyse a question that cannot be answered. When you become more depressed, you usually ask a lot of 'why?' questions. 'Why did I take those tablets?' or 'Why do I feel this way?' Another favourite is the 'if only . . .' fantasies, as in 'If only I felt better . . .'. Alternatively, you may be constantly comparing yourself unfavourably to others and making judgements and criticising yourself. Brooding invariably makes you feel more depressed because you never resolve the existing questions and may even generate new questions that cannot be answered. Try to avoid getting involved in these thoughts and practise switching your attention to the outside world.

Can you identify any brooding about your health (e.g. 'Why', 'If only . . . ')?

_____

_____

_____

Attention bias

When you are worried about your health, you become more self-focused on your physical sensations and feelings, and this tends to magnify the sensations. At the same time, you are discarding negative test results. This all tends to make you more aware of how you feel and makes you more likely to assume that your thoughts or the pictures in your mind (such as being ill) are realities. This, in turn, interferes with your ability to make simple decisions, pay attention to, or concentrate on, your normal tasks or what people around you are saying. You are likely to be less creative and less able to listen effectively. When severe, it may make you feel more paranoid. Your view of the world now depends on your thoughts and the way these chatter away inside your mind, rather than your experience. In other situations, you may be so focused on monitoring your physical sensations that you fail to take in the context and find it difficult to concentrate on what others are saying.

Can you identify any changes in your attention when you are focusing on your health?

_____

_____

_____

Avoidance behaviours

People with health anxiety use a variety of different mechanisms to cope – which usually makes the situation worse in the long term. When your fear is high, you may either try to distract yourself from your thoughts and feelings or try to escape from or avoid situations that remind you of illness or death. Here health anxiety becomes like an illness phobia, in which you fear developing the disease in the future. For example, you might avoid going to the doctor because you are convinced you will be given bad news. You might avoid people who are ill, hospitals, doctors' surgeries, funerals, cemeteries, or reading anything about illness or death in the media. In this respect, you may have so-called 'magical thinking', where you believe that simply thinking about bad events will make them happen.

Can you identify any avoidance behaviours in your health anxiety and the intention behind them?

_____

_____

_____

Checking

When your doubt is high, you may make excessive 'checks' in the form of self-examination. Examples include checking whether:

- you have a lump
- your heart rate is too fast or blood pressure is too high
- you are losing excessive weight
- your nervous system is still normal
- you are losing your memory

- your tremor is getting worse
- you can still swallow
- your skin blemish is changing.

You are likely to be checking for information on the internet or in books and in the media and going to your doctor. Checking is an example of a 'safety-seeking behaviour' that aims to prevent harm, increase certainty and a sense of control and reduce anxiety. People with health anxiety try to adopt ways to improve the way they feel, but unfortunately the solutions usually leave them feeling worse and prevent them from testing out their fears. Safety behaviours are a way of 'trying too hard' to prevent bad consequences but often the solutions become the problem. Needless to say, you must stop all your safety behaviours if you are to overcome your health anxiety successfully.

Can you identify any checking behaviours in your health anxiety and the intention behind them?

_____

_____

_____

Reassurance seeking

You may be seeking repeated reassurance from friends or your doctor to find out the cause of your symptoms. When you are dissatisfied by one doctor, you may seek a second and third opinion and so on. Each doctor may order a new set of tests. Some of these tests may have ambiguous findings, leading to further tests. You in turn may become very dismissive or dissatisfied with your doctors. Interestingly, doctors can become frustrated with people with health anxiety and may prefer to refer you on to another doctor (rather than a mental health professional). Health anxiety influences your friends and family, too, since when you are preoccupied with your health and are seeking reassurance you may appear disinterested in anything else and distant. This in turn may lead people to become frustrated and fed up with you or to keep away from you.

Can you identify any reassurance seeking or attempts to reassure yourself in your health anxiety?

_____

_____

_____

The contents of worries, safety behaviours and avoidance behaviours are closely related. When a person has to enter a situation that she or he normally avoids, then the safety behaviours start to reduce the potential for discomfort. You may then try to avoid thinking about it by distracting yourself from the thought.

Defining your problems

Coming up with a list of your problems helps in several ways. First, it helps you to break down your health anxiety into specific areas to tackle. It also gives you a chance to rate these problems now, overall, so that you can re-rate them later and so measure your progress.

Paul's fear of cancer problem list:

Severity rating: 0–10 (Where 0 is no problem and 10 is very severe)

1. Being very worried with a fear that I might develop cancer, leading me to think about it most of the day and repeatedly check my body and seek reassurance.

   Rating: 10

2. Feeling depressed, leading me to spend as much time as I can at home and not keeping on top of my bills and avoiding seeing my friends or doing any chores.

   Rating: 8

Now make your own list of problems and rate the severity of each one.

EXERCISE 3.1: PROBLEM LIST

Severity rating: 0–10 (Where 0 is no problem and 10 is very severe)

1 _____

_____

Rating: _____

2 _____

_____

Rating: _____

3 _____

_____

Rating: _____

4 _____

_____

Rating: _____

Describing your goals

Next, you need to write a description of your goals relating to the problems that you have described and the values you have identified. Start with short-term goals, which are easier to tackle, and set yourself a realistic timetable by which you intend to move on to the next set of goals.

SAMPLE GOAL LIST

Progress rating: 0–10 (Where 0 = no progress and 10 = total improvement)

GOALS	Progress rating
SHORT TERM	
1. To stop repeatedly checking my body and instead get to work on time	1
2. To stop investigating symptoms on the internet and instead spend at last an hour a day with my children.	8
MEDIUM TERM	
1. To resume my social life by meeting up with friends outside my home twice a week	3
2. To go to the gym three times a week	5
3. To go out to the local shopping centre once a week.	5
LONG TERM	
1. To be a good partner and spend time doing things together	3
2. To learn to play the piano and practise daily.	4

SAMPLE GOAL LIST

Try to make your own goals Specific, Measurable, Achievable, Realistic and within a Time frame (SMART goals).

Some individuals with health anxiety have forgotten what is normal or healthy. To help generate ideas for healthy alternative behaviours, consider the following questions:

- What did you do before you had health anxiety?
- If you had a twin, who was the same as you in every respect but without health anxiety, what would they do?
- What would a role model of yours do?
- What would someone who inspires you do?

You will need to ask yourself these questions for goals in the short, medium and long term. You can then monitor your progress towards your goals on a scale of zero to ten, where zero is no progress at all towards the goal and ten means the goal has been achieved and sustained. Remember to make sure that your goals relate to your valued directions in life and tackle what you have been avoiding.

EXERCISE 3.2: LIST OF GOALS

Progress rating: 0–10 (Where 0 = no progress and 10 = goal completely reached)

SHORT TERM

1 _____ ❏

2 _____ ❏

3 _____ ❏

MEDIUM TERM

1 _____ ❏

2 _____ ❏

3 _____ ❏

LONG TERM

1 _____ ❏

2 _____ ❏

3 _____ ❏

Focusing more on what's important to you, and less on health

Measuring your progress

Identifying and rating the current severity of your health anxiety at the outset will give you a reference point against which you can measure your progress. The questionnaire below is designed to help you define the nature of the problem and effect on your life. Most of the scales can be completed weekly or fortnightly to determine whether you are making progress or not.

The health anxiety inventory

This questionnaire was developed by Paul Salkovskis and colleagues and is widely used to measure the severity of health anxiety symptoms and change over time.

Each question consists of a group of four statements. Please read each group of statements carefully and then select the one that best describes your feelings over the past week. When you first start, it is probably appropriate to ask these questions about the last six months. When monitoring treatment, applying the scale questions to the last week is more usual. Identify the statement by ringing the letter next to it. For example, if you think that statement a) is correct, ring statement a). It may be that more than one statement applies, in which case please ring any that are applicable.

1 a)   I do not worry about my health.

  b)   I occasionally worry about my health.

  c)   I spend much of my time worrying about my health.

  d)   I spend most of my time worrying about my health.

2 a)   I notice aches/pains less than most other people (of my age).

  b)   I notice aches/pains as much as most other people (of my age).

  c)   I notice aches/pains more than most other people (of my age).

  d)   I am aware of aches/pains in my body all the time.

3 a)   As a rule I am not aware of bodily sensations or changes.

  b)   Sometimes I am aware of bodily sensations or changes.

  c)   I am often aware of bodily sensations or changes.

  d)   I am constantly aware of bodily sensations or changes.

4 a)   Resisting thoughts of illness is never a problem.

  b)   Most of the time I can resist thoughts of illness.

  c)   I try to resist thoughts of illness but am often unable to do so.

  d)   Thoughts of illness are so strong that I no longer even try to resist them.

5 a)   As a rule I am not afraid that I have a serious illness.

  b)   I am sometimes afraid that I have a serious illness.

  c)   I am often afraid that I have a serious illness.

  d)   I am always afraid that I have a serious illness.

6 a) I do not have images (mental pictures) of myself being ill.

 b) I occasionally have images of myself being ill.

 c) I frequently have images of myself being ill.

 d) I constantly have images of myself being ill.

7 a) I do not have any difficulty taking my mind off thoughts about my health.

 b) I sometimes have difficulty taking my mind off thoughts about my health.

 c) I often have difficulty in taking my mind off thoughts about my health.

 d) Nothing can take my mind off thoughts about my health.

8 a) I am lastingly relieved if my doctor tells me there is nothing wrong.

 b) I am initially relieved, but the worries sometimes return later.

 c) I am initially relieved, but the worries always return later.

 d) I am not relieved if my doctor tells me there is nothing wrong.

9 a) If I hear about an illness I never think I have it myself.

 b) If I hear about an illness I sometimes think I have it myself.

 c) If I hear about an illness I often think I have it myself.

 d) If I hear about an illness I always think I have it myself.

10 a) If I have a bodily sensation or change I rarely wonder what it means.

 b) If I have a bodily sensation or change I often wonder what it means.

 c) If I have a bodily sensation or change I always wonder what it means.

 d) If I have a bodily sensation or change I must know what it means.

11 a) I usually feel at very low risk of developing a serious illness.

b) I usually feel at fairly low risk of developing a serious illness.

c) I usually feel at moderate risk of developing a serious illness.

d) I usually feel at high risk of developing a serious illness.

12 a) I never think I have a serious illness.

b) I sometimes think I have a serious illness.

c) I often think I have a serious illness.

d) I usually think that I am seriously ill.

13 a) If I notice an unexplained bodily sensation I don't find it difficult to think about other things.

b) If I notice an unexplained bodily sensation I sometimes find it difficult to think about other things.

c) If I notice an unexplained bodily sensation I often find it difficult to think about other things.

d) If I notice an unexplained bodily sensation I always find it difficult to think about other things.

14 a) My family/friends would say I do not worry enough about my health.

b) My family/friends would say I have a normal attitude to my health.

c) My family/friends would say I worry too much about my health.

d) My family/friends would say I am a hypochondriac.

For the following questions, please think about what it might be like if you had a serious illness of a type which particularly concerns you (such as heart disease, cancer, multiple sclerosis and so on). Obviously, you cannot know for definite what it would be like; please give your best estimate of what you *think* might happen, basing your estimate on what you know about yourself and serious illness in general.

15 a) If I had a serious illness I would still be able to enjoy things in my life quite a lot.

   b) If I had a serious illness I would still be able to enjoy things in my life a little.

   c) If I had a serious illness I would be almost completely unable to enjoy things in my life.

   d) If I had a serious illness I would be completely unable to enjoy life at all.

16 a) If I developed a serious illness there is a good chance that modern medicine would be able to cure me.

   b) If I developed a serious illness there is a moderate chance that modern medicine would be able to cure me.

   c) If I developed a serious illness there is a very small chance that modern medicine would be able to cure me.

   d) If I developed a serious illness there is no chance that modern medicine would be able to cure me.

17 a) A serious illness would ruin some aspects of my life.

   b) A serious illness would ruin many aspects of my life.

   c) A serious illness would ruin almost every aspect of my life.

   d) A serious illness would ruin every aspect of my life.

18 a) If I had a serious illness I would not feel that I had lost my dignity.

   b) If I had a serious illness I would feel that I had lost a little of my dignity.

   c) If I had a serious illness I would feel that I had lost quite a lot of my dignity.

   d) If I had a serious illness I would feel that I had totally lost my dignity.

SCORING

Score 0 for items circled a), score 1 for items circled b), 2 for items circled c), 3 for items circled d). The total range is 0 to 54.

If you score 18 or more, you probably have health anxiety and may benefit from an assessment and treatment. You can also use the scale to measure your progress in a self-help programme, your work with a therapist or use of medication for health anxiety. A reliable improvement during treatment is a decrease of 4 or more points. If you manage to decrease to 17 or less at the end of the treatment, then you are likely to have recovered from health anxiety.

Source: This questionnaire is reproduced with permission from the main author. It was developed by P. Salkovskis, K. Rimes, H. Warwick and D. M. Clark (2002), 'The health anxiety inventory: development and validation of scales for the measurement of health anxiety and hypochondriasis', in *Psychological Medicine,* 32, 843–53.

Rating the impact of your health anxiety on your life

Another useful questionnaire to monitor your progress looks at the degree to which health anxiety interferes in your ability to do certain day-to-day tasks in your life. Look at each numbered section below and determine on the scale provided how much your problem impairs your ability to carry out the activity. Again, you can use this to measure your outcome during and after therapy.

Work and social functioning

1 WORK OR STUDY To what extent does your health anxiety interfere in your ability to work or study? (If you are retired or choose not to have a job for reasons unrelated to your problem, please write N/A (not applicable).

2 HOME MANAGEMENT To what extent does your health anxiety interfere in your home management (e.g. cleaning, tidying, shopping, cooking, looking after home/children, paying bills, etc.)?

3 SOCIAL LEISURE ACTIVITIES To what extent does your health anxiety interfere in your social life with other people (e.g. parties, pubs, outings, entertaining, etc.)?

4 PRIVATE LEISURE ACTIVITIES To what extent does your health anxiety interfere in your private leisure activities done alone (e.g. reading, gardening, sewing, hobbies, walking, etc.)?

| 0 | 1 | 2 | 3 | 4 | 5 | 6 | 7 | 8 |

Not at all   Slightly   Definitely   Markedly   Very severely

5 FAMILY AND RELATIONSHIPS To what extent does your health anxiety interfere in your ability to form and maintain close relationships with others including the people whom you live with?

| 0 | 1 | 2 | 3 | 4 | 5 | 6 | 7 | 8 |

Not at all   Slightly   Definitely   Markedly   Very severely

TOTAL OF 5 ITEMS =

4

Reclaiming your life

As you make headway in overcoming your health anxiety, you need to start thinking about how you're going to reclaim your life. This is important as part of helping focus your attention into areas of life other than your health. It's also important because 'health anxiety loves a vacuum'; any 'space' left in your life will tend to be filled by health anxiety if you are prone to it. Everyone needs some space in their lives, and many people find it very therapeutic to sit quietly and allow thoughts simply to pass through their minds without engaging with them. However, health anxiety can be a very time-consuming and energy-consuming problem, and research has shown that the extent to which people who are recovering from health anxiety absorb themselves into other activities can have a significant effect on their chances of relapsing.

Many people who have had health anxiety notice that aspects of their lives have been restricted or 'put on hold' because of their fears and rituals. Here are some areas of life to think about. Are there things you would like to do more of? Now is a good time to review what is important in your life using the Valued Directions exercise, which we describe below.

Much of health anxiety is the result of becoming overly focused on:

- your own health
- other people's health
- health in the media, or
- the place of health, illness and death in our culture.

The aim of the next exercise is to gain an understanding of your values or what you want your life to stand for. This will enable you to engage in a life that has a better balance and is less dominated by health. Once you know what your valued directions are, you can start moving towards them. To help you monitor whether you are in fact acting according to your values, we have prepared various tables and exercises for you to work through. There are various prompts for each area where you can write down a brief statement. You don't have to fill in a values statement for every area; just leave an area blank if you think it is inappropriate for you. After writing down your statements, you may want to clarify them with a friend or therapist. Be careful not to write down values that you think you should have just because others will approve of them. Only write down what you know to be true for yourself. It is probably a valued direction if you acted on it consistently before you experienced your health anxiety. If you have had a health anxiety for many years, you may struggle with this exercise, but you should persevere because it is very important.

Note that values are not goals – they are more like compass points, and they need to be lived out through committed action. Goals are part of the process of committing yourself to action. Goals are achievable – for example, you can get married, which is one goal – whereas values are more open-ended: with values, you never reach your destination because there is always something more you can do to work towards them, such as being a good partner. If your valued direction in life is to be a good parent, then your first goal might be to spend a few hours just hanging out with your son or daughter and playing with him or her. Other goals might be to get your son or daughter through school or college as part of the valued direction of being a good parent. This does not mean you will not fail at times – it means that, if you fail, you can learn from it, take responsibility, and restart your commitment to the action. It might take some time to discover all your values, so here are some prompts to help you:

- Imagine what aspects of life you would be engaging in if you were not feeling anxious or preoccupied with your health at this moment. We understand that you may feel upset at the things you seem to have lost, but this exercise will help you chart your course on the journey you wish to take.
- Brainstorm all the activities and interests you can think of and consider which might be close to your valued directions.
- Remind yourself of what you used to value or aspire to when you were younger. Have any of these values simply been 'squashed' by your health anxiety?

- Consider whether a fear of what other people will think, or a fear of failing, might be holding you back from pursuing your valued directions.
- Consider a role model or hero and the values he or she holds.
- Have a chat with a trusted friend (or therapist) who knows you well and see what he or she would guess your values to be.
- Be prepared to experiment and 'try on for size', living consistently with a given valued direction to see how it 'fits'.

The following form is adapted from Kelly Wilson's Values Worksheet.

SAMPLE VALUED DIRECTIONS FORM

Area	Valued direction
1 Intimacy (What is important to you in how you act in an intimate relationship? What sort of partner do you want to be? If you are not involved in a relationship at present, how would you like to act in a relationship?)	*I want to develop a relationship and be a good partner and spend time doing things together.*
2 Family relationships (What is important to you in how you want to act as a brother/sister; son/daughter; father/mother or parent-in-law? If you are not in contact with some of your family members, would you like to be and how would you act in such a relationship?)	*I'd like to be a good daughter and less dependent on my parents for support and to help them more in the future. I'd like to spend more time with my brother, getting to know him better.*

3 Social relationships (What is important to you in the way you act in the friendships you have? How would you like your friends to remember you? If you have no friends, would you like to have some and what role would you like in a friendship?)	*I'd like to be a good friend, more open and available to my friends.*
4 Work (What is important to you in your work? What sort of employee do you want to be? How important to you is what you achieve in your career? What sort of business do you want to run?)	*I'd like to return to work and be more approachable and help to make it a more successful company.*
5 Education and training (What is important to you in your education or training? What sort of student do you want to be? If you are not in education, would you like to be?)	*To improve my prospects of securing a better job in the future, I'd like to do more management and IT training.*
6 Recreation (What is important to you in what you do to follow any interests, sports or hobbies? If you are not following any interests, what would you ideally like to be pursuing?)	*I'd like to get back to playing tennis and swimming. I might like to learn to play a musical instrument.*
7 Spirituality (If you are spiritual, what is important to you in the way you want to follow a spiritual path? If you are not, would you like to be and what do you ideally want?)	*I'd like to learn more about Buddhism.*

8 Voluntary work (What would you like to do for the larger community? For example, voluntary or charity work or political activity?)	*I'd like to do more to help others in a charity for health anxiety or for obsessive compulsive disorder and raise money for them.*
9 Health/physical well-being (What is important to you in how you act for your physical health?)	*Eating a healthy diet and taking exercise.*
10 Mental health (What is important to you generally in how you look after your mental health?)	*I'd like to be better at managing my stress at the end of the working day.*

Now try to define your own valued directions in life.

EXERCISE 4.1: UNDERSTANDING YOUR VALUES

Area	Valued direction
1 Intimacy (What is important to you in how you act in an intimate relationship? What sort of partner do you want to be? If you are not involved in a relationship at present, how would you like to act in a relationship?)	
2 Family relationships (What is important to you in how you want to act as a brother/sister; son/daughter; father/mother or parent-in-law? If you are not in contact with some of	

your family members, would you like to be and how would you act in such a relationship?)	
3 Social relationships (What is important to you in the way you act in the friendships you have? How would you like your friends to remember you? If you have no friends, would you like to have some and what role would you like in a friendship?)	
4 Work (What is important to you in your work? What sort of employee do you want to be? How important to you is what you achieve in your career? What sort of business do you want to run?)	
5 Education and training (What is important to you in your education or training? What sort of student do you want to be? If you are not in education, would you like to be?)	
6 Recreation (What is important to you in what you do to follow any interests, sports or hobbies? If you are not following any interests, what would you ideally like to be pursuing?)	
7 Spirituality (If you are spiritual, what is important to you in the way you want to follow a spiritual path? If you are not, would you like to be and what do you ideally want?)	

8 Voluntary work (What would you like to do for the larger community? For example, voluntary or charity work or political activity?)	
9 Health/physical well-being (What is important to you in how you act for your physical health?)	
10 Mental health (What is important to you generally in how you look after your mental health?)	
11 Any other values that are not listed above	

Source: Adapted from the 'Valued Living Questionnaire', *Acceptance and Commitment Therapy* (Guilford Publications, 2004) by Steven Hayes, Kirk Strosahl and Kelly Wilson.

You might like to think of your life as a garden, where checking, worrying, safety-seeking and avoidance behaviours are the weeds that have taken root and probably grown over time. We hope that you will succeed in pulling up those weeds (sometimes even with the help of a little weedkiller in the form of medication) and will plant some desirable plants in the form of new or increased activities and interests and more helpful ways of coping. Now you need to think about maintaining the garden, which of course means continuing to 'pull up' safety-seeking and avoidance behaviours, worry and the catastrophic misinterpretations that maintain health anxiety. One of the best ways of reducing the chances of weeds growing back is to make sure you pull them up and get the roots out as well, otherwise part of the weed is left in the ground and can grow back again. The parts of health anxiety that are left in your life might be very subtle and something you can live with (such as 'mini' checks, slight avoidance, resisting certain thoughts). To reduce the chances of them growing into something bigger, especially under the 'right' conditions such as at times of stress, keep working to get rid of them. Alongside this, you'll need to take ongoing care of your new activities and attitudes to make sure they flourish.

Hobbies

What interest have you always wanted to take up but found that fears or lack of time have prevented you? Here is a small range of possibilities (in no particular order) to give you some ideas:

chess	tennis	football
dressmaking	sailing	walking
quizzes	baking	flower arranging
fishing	swimming	gardening
decorating	pottery	painting
jogging	wine tasting	cycling
motorsport	singing	languages
mechanics	squash	basketball
pets	enamelling	antiques
astronomy	jewellery making	cooking
martial arts	reading	writing
voluntary work	drama	meditation

Make a note here of any hobbies or interests that you think would be useful for you to try, reintroduce or do a bit more often.

_____

_____

_____

_____

_____

Work and education

Do you think that your health anxiety has interfered with your seeking work or studying? If you're in work, do you think your health anxiety has interfered with you advancing your career or changing careers? This is a common experience for people who have health anxiety. As you get better, start to set goals for how you would like to see your work life develop, and build a realistic and practical action plan for how you will move towards these goals.

Make a note here of any areas to develop in your career or education.

_____

_____

_____

_____

_____

Relationships

There is good evidence that a network of social support and a person in your life you can confide in helps to reduce the chances of your suffering from emotional problems in general. Improving your relationships, spending more time with other people and doing things you find enjoyable or worthwhile will also help fill the gap left by your health anxiety as you overcome it. Put simply, your relationships with other people are vitally important in keeping health anxiety at bay.

Improving your relationships

Consider how you would like things to be different in your relationships with other people. Who would you like to make things different with? For example:

- partner or spouse
- children
- relatives
- friends
- colleagues
- neighbours

Many of the changes in your relationships will happen naturally, as you become less preoccupied with your fears, and are more able to focus outside yourself and on the world around you. Good relationships are sustained by time, thought and effort. People recovering from health anxiety often find they have additional problems, though, such as their health anxiety having restricted the amount of time they've spent socialising, their drive for reassurance having shaped their conversations for years. Acting consistently with your personal values on the kind of friend/partner/ colleague/son/daughter etc. you'd like to be will help you restore more healthy relationships.

It's often said that the lifeblood of any relationship is communication. Keep in mind that we communicate not only by what we say, but also by the way we say things, when and where we say them, and by a variety of non-verbal methods (such as eye contact, body language, spending time, sharing experiences, a hug). Here are some tips to improve communication:

- If you have something important to discuss with someone, find a mutually good slot with enough time set aside for both of you to talk and listen.
- Use 'I feel' statements like 'I feel disappointed that we couldn't meet up last week' rather than blaming statements like 'You made me so angry'.
- If you want to give feedback to someone on their behaviour, keep it clear, brief and specific. Remember it's OK to give positive feedback like 'I'd really like to thank you for . . . ' as well as saying how you'd like things to be different – 'I'd really appreciate it if you could . . . '.
- If you've given someone some feedback, check how they feel and what they think of what you've said.

- Try to avoid getting stuck in the trap of thinking there is a right or 'true' way of doing something. Value the differences in others and seek a compromise if appropriate.
- Deal with critical remarks by finding some part of the criticism to agree with and invite the person to tell you more. This will enable you to evaluate the criticism effectively and respond in a non-defensive, self-accepting way, such as 'You're right, my health anxiety has made life more difficult for you. I've often worried about the effect it has had on you. What particularly would you like to be different?'

Make a note here of ways to develop a relationship or improve communication that you might benefit from.

_____

_____

_____

_____

_____

5

What causes health anxiety?

This chapter considers the development of health anxiety across your lifespan.

We do not know the exact 'cause' of health anxiety. However, we hope in this chapter to help you identify some of the pieces in the jigsaw and recognise that *understanding* your health anxiety is part of the solution. Also note that there will be several pieces in the jigsaw that are 'unknown' and that it is impossible to 'get to the bottom of it all'.

Before we help you achieve an understanding of your health anxiety, it's worth thinking about how our minds work in evolutionary terms. We want to acknowledge Professor Paul Gilbert for these insights.

All human beings could be said to have a design fault in the brain. There is a lot of evidence that we share an 'old brain' with reptiles and mammals. It is responsible for our emotions and drives. These help us to be safe, to find food and to reproduce. We also have the benefit of a well-developed 'new brain' which gives us considerably more sophisticated abilities. We talk more about the new brain and how it relates to the old brain below. It is important therefore to develop a good understanding of the motivation behind your behaviour, which is driven by your old brain as a way of trying to keep you safe.

The three main systems in our 'old brain' are:

1. The threat system. This is designed to motivate us to detect and respond to threats in our lives. We then feel the emotions of anxiety, disgust and anger and create the 'fight or flight' response. The threat system has become dominant in health anxiety.

2. The drive system. This is designed to motivate us to be interested in, and take pleasure from, obtaining important resources (e.g. food, sex, social approval). It enables us to survive, to experience pleasure and to feel excited. Some people try to cope with their health anxiety by keeping themselves busy and achieving things with their drive system. When this system is eventually overwhelmed by the threat system (as often occurs), they may feel depressed and lack any drive at all.

3. The compassion system. This is designed to motivate us to connect with others and to understand ourselves. It helps to balance the other two systems, giving us a feeling of well-being and contentment. This system may also be overwhelmed by the threat system in health anxiety and, if it is, you may struggle to self-soothe and connect with others. This is the basis of the compassion-focused therapy developed by Paul

Gilbert and colleagues that helps you to balance the threat and drive systems.

For now, we will focus on the threat system in health anxiety. To begin to understand anxiety, let's scroll back thousands of years and imagine the inhabitants of the African savannah – the ones that survived had a good threat system that kept them safe when there was a danger such as a lion in the vicinity. You will probably recognise the response they will have experienced: feelings of anxiety and panic coupled with the body automatically preparing to fight, flee or freeze. The threat system works rapidly to give the best chance of safety and survival. There is no time to take unnecessary risks. To survive, you need a good functioning threat system.

In health anxiety, the threats are not external (a lion, a mugger, a vehicle out of control); they are internal, in our minds, and come from the 'new brain' which is well developed and responsible for our ability to problem solve, to plan, to use language and to be creative. It is both invaluable – enabling us to figure out how to get to the moon or create a work of art – and our Achilles' heel as it allows us to *imagine* threats. So, a tricky loop can appear between the 'new brain' and the 'old brain': the new brain tries to be rational and convince the old brain that the fasciculation in your muscle or the heart palpitation is not a threat. Unfortunately, as the threat system is designed to keep you safe, when you are anxious it tends to dominate ('Better safe than sorry'). So, when you 'imagine' a threat, it activates the system in just the same way as a real external threat would. That's why it feels as if you have two parts to your mind – your anxious old brain and your rational new brain. The key issue is that all humans need a good threat system to survive – anxiety is a normal response, which you can't get rid of. You will be learning to understand the context in which your threat system is being activated, and the processes involved, so that you can try to distance yourself and act against the way you feel.

Factors that make up health anxiety

When trying to understand your health anxiety, it is usually helpful to consider factors under each of these three headings

(a) Circumstances that have made you vulnerable to developing health anxiety

(b) Things that have triggered your health anxiety, and

(c) Things that maintain your health anxiety (or keep it going).

There may be different types of health anxiety, which makes it more complicated.

A good understanding of the development of your health anxiety can help you to take a more sympathetic, compassionate view of yourself. Your efforts to overcome it will then be more effective. We will cover what *maintains* your health anxiety in the next chapter.

We can confidently say that health anxiety, like all disorders of the mind, results from a combination of biological, psychological, social and cultural factors. Different combinations of such factors may give rise to similar symptoms in various individuals, which adds to the difficulty in understanding why health anxiety develops. While the precise risk factors relevant to a particular individual are often unclear, this does not alter the current treatment. One person's health anxiety may be caused *mainly* by genetic or biological factors, whereas another may arise *mainly* from psychological or social factors. At one extreme, a young person with a strong genetic predisposition to anxiety may find that a relatively 'normal' event like an early death of a relative may trigger their symptoms of health anxiety. At the other extreme, an individual may develop health anxiety after a major illness which they have recovered from physically. One way of thinking about the various contributions that biological, life experiences and psychological factors make to various cases of health anxiety is to imagine them like glasses of liquid. They are all full to the same extent, but the ingredients vary according to each individual.

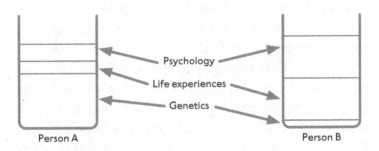

We explained at the beginning of the chapter that just being human lays you open to developing health anxiety. Crocodiles or elephants do not worry about whether they are going to get motor neurone disease or cancer. People who are very intelligent or creative seem to do worse with health anxiety and spend more time researching information about possible illness.

Factors that can make you vulnerable to health anxiety include your genes or an anxious temperament. Scientists find that studying identical twins helps to add to our knowledge of illness more easily than comparing individuals with different DNA. In twin studies, up to 40 per cent of health anxiety is thought to be heritable – like any other mental disorder. This does not mean you cannot overcome health anxiety. It just means you may be predisposed to developing health anxiety. It's not your fault you are born human with certain genes that might predispose you. It's just bad luck. Close family members will not necessarily know that another member of the family or previous generations are (or were) more likely to be anxious or worriers. Also, the symptoms may be mild or may have passed many years ago. Some researchers believe that a younger member of the family may copy another's behaviour, which may be another influence on the development of health anxiety.

Genes usually require life experiences to 'switch on' their health anxiety, and, in different or better circumstances, the person concerned might never have developed health anxiety. Life experiences might include adversity during childhood or adolescence, such as emotional neglect, abuse or bullying that create chronic stress. A child may learn from the media or from their friends about deaths from a germ. The child then builds a narrative in their minds that makes them more alert and vigilant for signs of illness. Childhood experiences include learning from your carers that minor bodily changes (i.e. feeling unwell) are unusual and need extra attention. Your carers may have been very overprotective. Equally they may have been emotionally or physically abusive or neglectful. One or more of your carers may have had a serious illness or died young. You can imagine there are all sorts of influences that may have shaped your beliefs and your approach to illness.

Triggers for health anxiety

Health anxiety can begin gradually or suddenly. Factors that might trigger or 'switch on' health anxiety are poorly understood. A significant proportion of people with health anxiety seem to experience no specific triggers, though, and you may be amongst them. Individuals with health anxiety are more likely than those unaffected to have had one or more life events in the six months before the onset of their health anxiety. These can be happy events such as marriage or the birth of a baby, stressful ones such as change of job or moving to a new house, or distressing ones such as bereavement or homelessness. Occasionally, taking stimulant drugs such as cocaine or amphetamines may have triggered or aggravated health anxiety. In such cases, health anxiety usually improves when the drug is stopped, but not necessarily.

A major event such as a serious illness or accident in yourself or a loved one, or an experience such as nearly dying, may 'switch on' or aggravate health anxiety. The kind of images which haunt the thoughts of people with health anxiety are often associated with memories of bad experiences, which they may not have been able to process emotionally. Health anxiety symptoms may therefore be maintained by an emotional memory that is conditioned to a sensation or medical procedure. This is a promising area on which to target treatment. If we can update the 'ghosts from the past', the memories lose their sense of 'nowness'. This can be done with an approach called imagery rescripting or EMDR (Eye Movement Desensitisation and Reprocessing). If you believe this is the case, it's worth discussing with a therapist.

Psychological factors in the development of health anxiety

Some people with health anxiety would say they have always been a worrier. For some people, they will over-estimate the degree of risk and the need for certainty. Other developmental factors that may contribute to the development of health anxiety are using avoidance to cope with uncomfortable thoughts and feelings, trying to control thoughts and over-analysing (called ruminating). In anxiety, there is an attention bias towards potential threat (including upon your own mind and body). As we've noted earlier, our brain's threat system has a 'better safe than sorry' bias.

However, in the case of health anxiety too much safety can very definitely make you sorry.

Your brain is overloaded because you think that you can prevent awful events from occurring and are extremely anxious about all the catastrophes that could occur and want to know for certain what is going to happen. Our assumption is that your brain is coping the best way it can to re-stabilise itself and reduce anxiety. This is reflected in abnormal brain scans, which can be regarded as the mind desperately trying to re-stabilise and to calm down. In the next chapter, we will focus on a psychological understanding of health anxiety. This explores the factors that maintain health anxiety – things you can change. We shall also discuss making changes in your family and social environment, which can be just as important.

Tying it all up

Here is an example from Anne, whom we introduced earlier:

(a) Circumstances that have made me vulnerable to developing health anxiety and how these relate to my motivation to prevent illness:

There is family history of anxiety in one of my grand-parents. I have always been a bit of a worrier and my mum was quite overprotective. She died from cancer when I was in my twenties.

(b) Things that have triggered or shaped my health anxiety:

It seemed like life was going quite well and I felt quite a lot of responsibility to make sure that my health didn't mess it up. I was also doing a lot of googling around COVID-19 and hearing/reading a lot of conflicting information and began to doubt whether health experts really know what they are doing.

Now you try

Try to summarise below or on a separate sheet of paper some of the developmental factors that have contributed to your health anxiety – perhaps some heritability with a family history of an emotional disorder, or feeling you were different or being bullied when you were a child. Have some of these developmental factors contributed to specific motivations such as an intolerance of uncertainty, or behaviours you use to try to control your thoughts and feelings?

(a) Circumstances that have made me vulnerable to developing health anxiety (e.g. heritability; childhood illnesses; early deaths of carers; attitude of my carers to illness) and how these relate to my motivation to prevent illness and avoid disability or death:

_____

_____

_____

_____

_____

(b) Things that have triggered or shaped my health anxiety
(e.g. sudden death of a relative):

_____

_____

_____

_____

_____

_____

Key points:

- You are *not* responsible for causing your health anxiety, and the exact causes of the condition are not completely clear.
- You may have been born more likely to develop health anxiety because of your genes.
- Your life experiences, since you were a child, may have influenced your mind to be more likely to develop health anxiety. Developing intolerance of uncertainty, being overly cautious, magical thinking

or trying to control your thoughts, checking, seeking reassurance and avoidance are all important processes that now maintain health anxiety.

- You may have had an experience (or combination of experiences) that triggered the onset of your health anxiety, such as a distressing event: for example, an unexpected death or where there has been a lot of uncertainty. For some readers this may be many years ago.
- We were all born with a brain that is rather focused on keeping us safe and needs our help to keep it healthy. Considering our 'tricky brain', it's not surprising that psychological problems like health anxiety are so common.
- Building a personalised understanding of the causes of your health anxiety can help you to be kinder and more understanding of your problem and begin to clarify what you need to change.

6

Understanding what's maintaining your health anxiety

As with solving most problems, you'll do a better job if you've defined the problem well. This chapter aims to help you understand the psychological processes that keep your health anxiety going. For clarity, we've loosely divided this into behavioural factors and thinking factors, but the two are very much related. For example, the more intolerant of uncertainty about your health you are, the more you're likely to check your body. However, it's also true that the more you check your body or seek reassurance, the more you reduce your mind's ability to tolerate doubt – a bit like a muscle that weakens through lack of use.

A key part of the maintenance of your health anxiety is the way you may be habitually interpreting normal sensations (like dizziness, tiredness) as evidence of a severe illness. This process, called 'catastrophising' or 'catastrophic misinterpretation', means you might interpret a 'safe' sensation such as a headache (caused by tension) as evidence of a brain tumour. Not surprisingly, if you believe this intrusive thought (when it is not true), you will make yourself feel more anxious. Some people experience intrusive thoughts and images about death or severe illness without any obvious trigger. Again, if you habitually view such intrusions as being important in the here and now, then it's not surprising that you will make yourself feel anxious. Another main factor in how health anxiety is maintained is understanding the way that some of your attempts to relieve yourself of anxiety (e.g. checking or looking for reassurance) are the very things that are keeping it going.

My solutions are the problem is a phrase we very much want you to keep in mind when you consider what is keeping your health anxiety going. By this we mean that we hope you'll come to understand that the strategies you've come to use to try to reduce your uncertainty and anxiety about your health are fuelling your worry. They are very understandable ways of coping with intrusive thoughts about a health problem, but the key question is: how helpful are they?

Your solutions might appear to work at first in that they reduce anxiety in the short term. Their aim is to increase the feeling of certainty and influence over events. Yet while you may feel that they are working at first, gradually they increase preoccupation and distress. They can produce new sensations, fuel doubt and increase the sense of feeling out of control.

As time goes by, you may become more depressed. Your friends and family might end up taking on your responsibilities. This in turn creates another feedback loop in which you lose your confidence and feel incapable of doing certain things. You may miss out on meaningful, enjoyable events and opportunities. Avoidance stops you from doing what is important to you. For example, you want to be a person to whom your friends and family can turn for support, or you want to be a good mother or father. When you can't do these things, you will inevitably feel more depressed. You might spend more time focusing on yourself and beating yourself up, and you find that you cannot act in a way that is important to you. Your behaviour then influences the people around you. Others may be critical or unsupportive and you will probably become more depressed, caught in a vicious circle.

Identifying your solutions that might be the problem

With strategies like checking your body for signs of illness, or looking possible symptoms up on the internet, there's an additional problem; if you go looking for trouble you might very well find it. You might 'find' something that appears to be an indication of a problem, and this fuels your worry. However, if you did not have health anxiety, you would not have noticed and it would have done you no harm. The table below gives some more examples.

TABLE 6.1: 'The solution is the problem'

Worry	Way of Coping	Unintended Consequences
I have AIDS	Getting more information on the internet	Increases doubt and uncertainty; generates more questions to research
I have stomach cancer	Seeking more medical opinions and investigations	Makes the concern seem more real; increases doubt; generates more false trails; makes me less able to tolerate doubt
I have a brain tumour	Self-reassurance	Increases doubt and uncertainty; generates more questions to research
I'm going to have a heart attack	Reviewing past reassurances	Increases my preoccupation and doubt and makes me less interested in my values
Thoughts of illness and death	Trying to push the thoughts out of my mind	Increases the number of distressing thoughts. Makes them more intrusive and I cannot generate new information
I'm going to die of breast cancer	Try to replace bad thoughts with happy thoughts	Increases the number of distressing

		thoughts. Makes them more intrusive and I cannot generate new information
I'm going to get a degenerative nerve disease from toxic chemicals	Avoiding or escaping from new or threatening situations or activities	Cannot generate new information; increases my fear of illness; feel more depressed as I come to realise that avoidance does not work
What if I've got motor neurone disease?	Monitoring my arms and legs for twitches or numbness	Can be very time-consuming and distracting. I notice twitches or numbness that I would probably otherwise barely notice. I'm only able to relax when it seems that all is fine, but I often feel drawn to check again
What if this lump means I've got cancer?	Checking my body for lumps	I keep finding parts of my body that feel like they could be a lump and it really freaks me out. I often then lose a lot of time searching the internet to try and work out if I should be worried

I'm losing my mind	Monitoring my mind for strange thoughts or sensations	Even the fact I'm doing this makes me feel like I'm losing it. I now feel like I don't really know what's normal anymore

Now please make a note of the strategies that you currently use that might be part of maintaining your own health anxiety. These might be things that you identify as actions you might not take (or at least not as often) if you were not so worried about your health.

Checking (e.g. your body, the internet)

_____

_____

_____

Reassurance seeking (e.g. re-playing past reassurance in your mind, re-reading doctors' letters)

_____

_____

_____

Things you avoid because of your fears about your health (e.g. certain foods, exercise, medical TV shows, avoiding touching parts of your body, or not allowing certain parts of your body to be touched)

_____

_____

_____

Attention bias (e.g. mentally scanning your body for any sensations that might be a sign of illness, paying too much attention to medical news stories)

_____

_____

_____

You can use the list you've made here to help you build your 'vicious flower' (vicious circles put together) later in this chapter.

Don't take our word for it

You might well be sceptical about this 'solutions are the problem' idea, since naturally you've been trying to help yourself, and much of what you've done is only common sense. Take reassurance, for example. Doctors are in fact trained to give reassurance, so it seems reasonable for them to give it and for you to seek it – right? Except that health anxiety is a *preoccupation that persists despite medical reassurance.* This means that it's crucial you try treating your problem as if it's a worry about a health problem rather than an actual or possible health problem.

If you are not convinced that safety behaviours make things worse, try a 'real-life' behavioural experiment.

- Spend one day dealing with your health anxiety the usual way and record the degree of distress and amount of time you spent in that day preoccupied with your health anxiety.
- Spend the next day increasing the frequency and duration of a safety behaviour, or double it if you can.
- The following day, go back to your usual way and repeat the above.

Take a look at the results of your four-day experiment. What do you make of them? Most people discover that the harder they try to seek reassurance, or increase their checking, the worse their preoccupation and feelings about their health are.

Common 'thinking styles' in health anxiety

When you feel anxious and preoccupied about the idea that you have a medical problem, you may experience both thoughts and images related to your concern.

In common with other emotional problems, health anxiety will drive your thinking in a negative and extreme direction. When there is an actual threat, like a lion that you need to escape from, your way of thinking can help to keep you safe ('Better safe than sorry'). However, it is unhelpful when there is no actual threat. This unhelpful way of thinking will in turn make you feel worse and influence what you focus upon and what you do. It thus plays a key role in maintaining your problem and leads to significant handicap ('Better to miss lunch than be lunch').

Two of the founding fathers of cognitive behavioural therapy, Albert Ellis and Aaron Beck, both identified particular patterns of thinking linked with emotional problems. The great advantage of knowing the ways in which your thinking might be affected by your health anxiety is that you can more readily spot a negative thought and learn to take these thoughts (and images) with a huge pinch of salt. Think of it as health anxiety propaganda, aiming to keep you preoccupied and distressed. Just as people during the Second World War had to learn to ignore the Nazi propaganda (aimed at lowering their morale) that invaded their radios, so you can learn to notice unhelpful thoughts without believing them to be true.

Here are some of the more common types of thinking styles that arise in health anxiety. It will be important to learn these so you can label your own 'thinking style'. While metaphors (like propaganda, spam emails, harassment by a bully, and so on) can be helpful as a reminder not to automatically believe our thoughts, it's important to remember that your brain is trying to help keep you safe – so don't be too hard on it!

Catastrophising

This is a key process in health anxiety when you interpret the physical sensations or health information in a catastrophic manner. This means jumping to the worst possible conclusion. For example:

heart skipping a beat	I'm going to have a heart attack
lumps under the skin	I've got cancer
tingling or numbness	I've got multiple sclerosis
headache	I've got a brain tumour
feeling run down	I'm dying

Can you give an example of the way you interpret your physical sensations and catastrophise?

_____

_____

_____

Overgeneralising

This means drawing too general a conclusion about something. An example in health anxiety is people losing confidence in healthcare services, doctors or other healthcare professionals. Sometimes difficult or distressing things happen, and of course mistakes are sometimes made. Thankfully, these are the exceptions rather than the norm and it does not mean it would happen to you. If you or someone you care about has had a bad experience, it's important not to 'throw the baby out with the bathwater' and to try to preserve your faith that if you became ill help would be at hand.

Can you give an example of the way you experience overgeneralising?

_____

_____

_____

Thought action fusion

This refers to the way thoughts and images are treated as if they are facts. For example, you might have a thought or image of yourself dying alone from AIDS and then treat this as a fact. Or you might interpret the image as being a sign of what the future holds.

Can you give an example of the way you experience thought action fusion?

_____

_____

_____

All-or-nothing (black-or-white) thinking

This is common in anxiety and refers to thinking in extreme, all-or-nothing terms. For example: 'I am either totally free from disease' or 'If I am ill, then I will soon experience a slow, painful death'.

Can you give an example of the way you think in an all-or-nothing thinking style in your health anxiety?

_____

_____

_____

Fortune-telling

This relates to catastrophising and refers to making negative and pessimistic predictions about the future. For example: 'I know I'll never get over this. I'm bound to end up dying alone. It's inevitable that my children will be terribly distressed for the rest of their lives if I die and leave them without a father/mother.'

Can you give an example of fortune-telling in your health anxiety? It could be a thought or an image.

_____

_____

_____

Mind reading

This refers to jumping to conclusions about what other people are thinking about you. For example: 'my doctor didn't look me in the eye because he knows there is something seriously wrong with me', or 'I know she said all was well, but I think the nurse knew I was anxious and just wanted to reassure me'.

Can you give an example of mind reading in your health anxiety?

_____

_____

_____

Disqualifying the positive

This refers to discounting positive information or twisting a positive into a negative. For example: 'The doctor said I was fine, but I think he may have been tired and not concentrating properly. There's no point in enjoying life if you know that one day you'll die.'

Can you give an example of the way you disqualify the positive in your health anxiety?

_____

_____

_____

Labelling

This is globally defining yourself. For example: 'I'm vulnerable in my health, I'm fragile, I'm defective.'

Can you give an example of the way you globally label your 'self' in your health anxiety?

_____

_____

_____

Emotional reasoning

This means making decisions based on listening too much to how you feel or your 'gut' instead of looking at the objective facts. For example: 'I know there's something wrong with me, I can just feel it. There must be something wrong otherwise I wouldn't feel so anxious.'

Can you give an example of the way you experience emotional reasoning in your health anxiety?

_____

_____

_____

Personalising

This refers to taking an event or someone's behaviour too personally. For example: 'the way the newsagent looked at me when he handed me my magazine was because he knows I'm ill'.

Can you give an example of the way you personalise information in your health anxiety?

_____

_____

_____

Magical or superstitious thinking

In health anxiety, there is sometimes an overlap with the magical thinking that can occur in obsessive compulsive disorder. An example is thinking that if you pass a hospice and think about people dying from cancer, then it will happen to you.

Do you have an example of magical thinking in your health anxiety?

_____

_____

_____

Intolerance of uncertainty

A key factor in health anxiety is the *intolerance of uncertainty*. This is the distress experienced in response to the yet *unknown* aspects of your symptoms (e.g. is it cancer or just a benign lump, or is it treatable if it is cancer?).

We cope better with *known* threats or disasters. So, if you know for certain that you have cancer, then you can start to prepare for it and get more information about how it will be treated. The problem for many people with health anxiety is finding it hard to tolerate not knowing whether they have nothing to worry about or if they have a very unlikely serious illness.

Donald Rumsfeld, the US Defence Secretary, described 'not knowing' in a news briefing about the limitations of intelligence reports for the Iraq War in 2002:

> *As we know, there are known knowns; these are things we know we know. We also know there are known unknowns; that is to say, we know there are some things we do not know. But there are also unknown unknowns – the ones we don't know we don't know.*

There are two dimensions of unknowns: 1) degree of awareness of events (your awareness that something exists), and 2) degree of knowledge of events (how much you know about that thing).

- 'Known knowns' are things that are known and predictable. Thus, we know for certain that we are going to die, and while we are alive we must pay taxes. A person who can accept these knowns will have quietly done the things they can to prepare for known events (e.g. make a will or prepare their annual tax submission).

- 'Known unknowns' are things that we are aware of but do not know whether they are going to occur. In health anxiety, not knowing whether you might develop motor neurone disease is more distressing than knowing for certain that you will develop it. So, we may have some facts about what might happen, but don't know exactly what will happen – there is ambiguity or uncertainty.

- 'Unknown unknowns' are things that are so unexpected or unforeseeable that they cannot be known about in advance. Thus, typewriter manufacturers in the 1950s could not predict that their business would be wiped out within forty years.

- Lastly, 'unknown knowns' were not described by Donald Rumsfeld, but this is where we know something for certain (e.g. that we are going to die or pay taxes), but deny it or do not want to think about it. We avoid anything to do with thinking about possible bad outcomes. This can occur in health anxiety.

So, the distress of 'not knowing' whether something bad is going to happen is often worse than the distress experienced when something bad is known to be happening. When there is an intolerance of uncertainty, there is a common response of worry (trying to work out what will happen or seeking reassurance about what might happen). The motivation is trying to reduce the distress of not knowing. Sometimes it seems to work in the short term, but it then strengthens the doubt and makes you more likely to check and seek reassurance again.

Sometimes people who experience anxiety try to make their life feel safer and more predictable as part of an understandable effort to reduce their overall levels of stress. For example, you might try to prevent uncertainty in everyday life by avoiding surprises. You may like order and always follow the same routines. However, this means you may become less and less flexible and less receptive to uncertainty, which can ultimately mean more discomfort.

What do you find it difficult to 'not know' in your health anxiety, and where do you feel your distress? (e.g. in your tummy).

_____

_____

_____

What did you do to reduce the distress (e.g. either avoid and under-engage with the problem) or over-engage (e.g. seek reassurance, check) or make a decision impulsively?

_____

_____

_____

We will return to the intolerance of uncertainty later in the book as it's a crucial process in health anxiety.

Attention bias

When people are anxious about something they tend to be especially vigilant, looking out for examples of whatever is worrying them. This is one of the helpful aspects of anxiety, should we be in a genuinely threatening situation. For example, it's helpful to be watchful if we are at risk of being attacked by a wild animal. Our attention becomes very narrow in observing where the animal is and what its next move is going to be.

In the same way, if you have been pregnant or have wanted to become pregnant, you may have noticed that suddenly the world seemed to be flooded with pregnant women and babies. How about if you (or someone you know) have just bought a new car? Have you found that you kept noticing the same make on the road? It's not that there are more babies being born or more cars of the same model being bought; it's just that our attention is seeking out the subjects that interest us: it is *biased towards* noticing those subjects. What is on our minds will influence what we notice; it's just part of how the human brain works.

How about someone who is anxious about spiders or insects? Have you ever observed that they tend to see them where and when you hadn't noticed anything? When people are anxious about something they tend to be more *vigilant* for examples of it.

In health anxiety this *attention bias* is one of the factors that keeps the condition going. For example:

- People who focus their attention internally on how they 'feel', and on illness-related information, will tend to magnify their anxiety, and sensations will become noticed at progressively lower thresholds. These include normal bodily sensations, for example of your heart racing or shortness of breath, or previously unnoticed features (like hair loss).
- People who focus on their intrusive thoughts and ideas will find these tend to be magnified and appear more frequently.
- It's not unusual for people who are particularly pre-occupied to even misread words that are close to the names of the illnesses they are afraid of; 'Chaucer St' becomes 'Cancer St'.
- Being vigilant for information about illness can lead to the sense that your feared illness is at near epidemic proportion.

Being self-focused means being on the outside looking back at yourself. It means being very aware of your thoughts, feelings, mental images and body sensations. Being focused on life means being on the inside and looking out at the world around you and at what you can touch, taste, feel, see, hear or smell. People with health anxiety are frequently self-focused and constantly monitoring their body or mind for possible symptoms of their feared illness.

Self-focused attention can also have a big effect on your overall mood. Spending a lot of time going over problems in your thoughts serves only to heighten stress on your mind and body. Refocusing your attention onto the outside world gives your brain a rest and allows you to take in what the world has to offer. Overcoming health anxiety will mean broadening your attention to take everything in, not just focusing on your body or mind, and refocusing your attention away from your inner world.

EXERCISE 6.1: WHAT DO YOU FOCUS ON?

Take a moment to consider the past day or past week, and try to identify what you tend to notice more of than the average person in the street. Do you monitor your thoughts, images or body sensations or part of your body? Do you look out for threats and dangers?

I'm over-aware of _____

1 _____

2 _____

3 _____

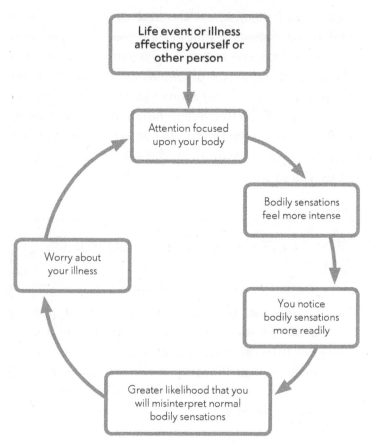

Figure 6.1 Vicious cycle of attention bias

Biased attention fuels biased conclusions

For example, if you constantly monitor the world and yourself for illness, you will see the world as a potentially dangerous place and yourself as vulnerable. If you are very tuned in to your body, its lumps, bumps, physical sensations and mental sensations, you are far more likely to jump to a conclusion that there's something wrong if you notice a minor change. This means you might experience distressing anxiety about a physical experience that the average person on the street might not have even noticed. We hope that this understanding helps you to see the benefit of learning to re-direct and become more flexible in where you focus your attention rather than it being frequently hijacked by your health anxiety. The remainder of this chapter focuses upon identifying the thoughts and beliefs that drive you to over-focus your attention on your body and health, and how to re-train your attention back on to the outside world.

Correcting your attention bias:

- Practise being absorbed in a particular task (like having a conversation), or the sights, tastes, smells, sounds and physical sensations of the world around you.
- When you notice your attention is drawn towards something you are monitoring to reduce risk, deliberately refocus your attention away from it on to something else around you.
- Similarly, if you tend to focus all the time on how you feel or on the harm you believe you might cause, refocus attention outside yourself on some practical tasks in hand or on the environment around you.

Thought suppression

One way you might be trying to avoid experiencing unpleasant thoughts or images of illness or death is to try to suppress them. However, suppressing thoughts will also bring unintended consequences; it has the effect of increasing the frequency of those thoughts, making you feel worse – trying not to think of something increases rather than decreases its intrusiveness. Try the following exercise.

Thought suppression illustration

The pink elephant experiment

Close your eyes and imagine a pink elephant. Now try very hard not to think of pink elephants for a minute; try to push any images of pink elephants out of your mind.

What did you notice was the effect of trying not to think of pink elephants?

Most people who do this exercise find that all they can think of is pink elephants. In research, this effect is called the 'white bear effect', from studies showing that when participants were asked not to think of white bears, they had more thoughts about them. Understanding the apparent upside-down way in which the human mind works is a key to understanding one of the processes in health anxiety. Very many people with this problem are caught in the trap of trying too hard to rid themselves of thoughts and doubts, and in fact this brings about the very opposite of what they want. Still not convinced that trying to get rid of intrusive thoughts, images or doubts makes them worse? Try a more 'real life' experiment.

Real life thought suppression experiment

a) Spend one day dealing with your thoughts in the usual way and record their frequency and the distress they cause you.
b) Spend the next day trying even harder to get rid of your thoughts and record their frequency and the distress they cause you. Try as hard as you can to suppress them.
c) The following day go back to your usual way of dealing with your negative thoughts, and then the next day return to step (b).

Look at the results of your four-day experiment. What do you make of them? Most people discover that their thoughts become more frequent and disturbing the harder they try to get rid of them. Stop trying so hard not to have the thought or image that's bothering you and it will bother you much less!

Putting it together: the vicious flower of health anxiety

The 'vicious flower', with its vicious circles (or 'petals'), is a way of visually illustrating to yourself the maintaining factors of your health anxiety. When you draw your vicious flower, the aim is to clarify connections between the way you cope when you feel anxious and the *effect* of the way you cope in maintaining the problem. The first half of each petal represents an 'output' of health anxiety such as a checking behaviour, or self-focused attention. The second half is the unintended consequence that follows and feeds back into the maintenance of health-anxious preoccupation. Keep in mind the concept that 'the solution is the problem'.

For example, if you check your body closely for signs of disease you might suffer from the problem of 'if you go looking for trouble, you'll find it'; you might find a mark on your skin, a lump on your body, a mental sensation, a bodily sensation that you would otherwise never have noticed and which would not have caused you harm. We have many, perfectly safe, medically unexplained, physical experiences that our brain would usually ignore. Some people use checking one side of their body against the other as a sort of test for whether something is abnormal (e.g. does one breast or one leg feel the same as the other). The problem is that our bodies aren't perfectly symmetrical, so this can, again, give you the impression that you might have detected a problem where none exists.

Here are some worked examples of vicious flowers to help illustrate the process.

Building your own vicious flower

The vicious flower is a way of combining a series of vicious circles to build a fuller picture of how your problem works. Here are the steps to building one:

1. Pick a recent, good example of your anxiety being triggered.
2. Note the main bodily sensation or movement that occurred at the time.
3. In the centre of the flower put the following:

   - How you interpreted the bodily sensation, what the doubt meant to you, or the process involved (catastrophising or wanting to know for certain)
   - Any images or difficult memories that are associated with the sensation
   - The emotion(s) (e.g. anxiety, shame, depression) that you felt
   - Further sensations of anxiety

This is represented in the vicious circle and is a bit like a panic attack, in the sense that these factors interact very quickly. This is technically called 'associative conditioning'.

Now examine each petal of the flower. Each one represents a way of coping that works in the short term (for example it reduces the doubt or distress in the middle of the flower), but the unintended consequences then feed the heart of the flower.

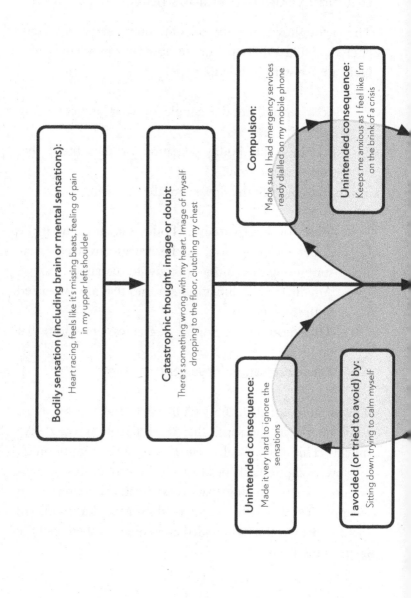

Bodily sensation (including brain or mental sensations):
Heart racing, feels like it's missing beats, feeling of pain in my upper left shoulder

Catastrophic thought, image or doubt:
There's something wrong with my heart. Image of myself dropping to the floor, clutching my chest

Compulsion:
Made sure I had emergency services ready dialled on my mobile phone

Unintended consequence:
Keeps me anxious as I feel like I'm on the brink of a crisis

Unintended consequence:
Made it very hard to ignore the sensations

I avoided (or tried to avoid) by:
Sitting down, trying to calm myself

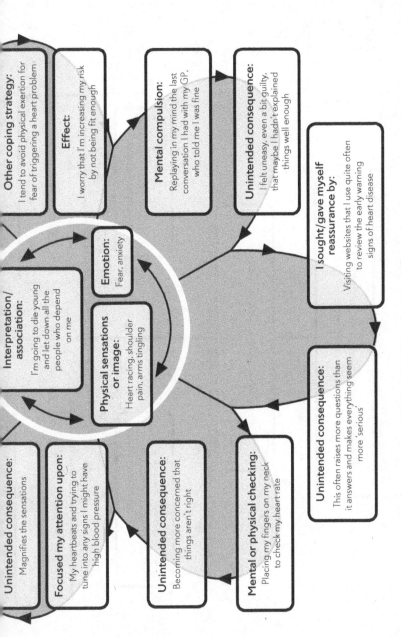

Figure 6.2 Adrian's vicious flower

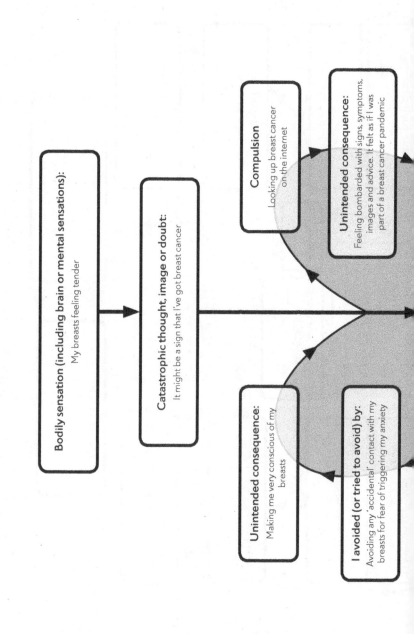

Bodily sensation (including brain or mental sensations):
My breasts feeling tender

Catastrophic thought, image or doubt:
It might be a sign that I've got breast cancer

Compulsion
Looking up breast cancer on the internet

Unintended consequence:
Feeling bombarded with signs, symptoms, images and advice. It felt as if I was part of a breast cancer pandemic

Unintended consequence:
Making me very conscious of my breasts

I avoided (or tried to avoid) by:
Avoiding any 'accidental' contact with my breasts for fear of triggering my anxiety

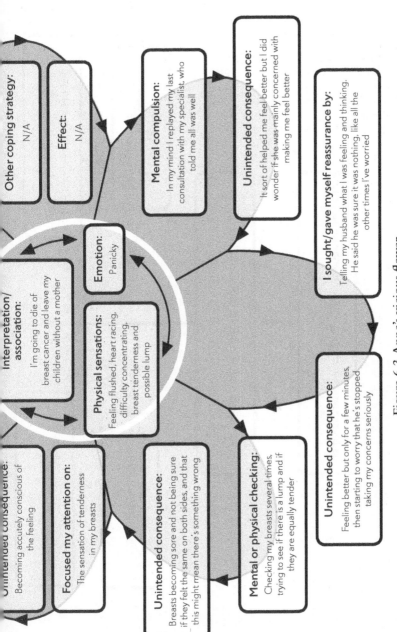

Figure 6.3 Anne's vicious flower

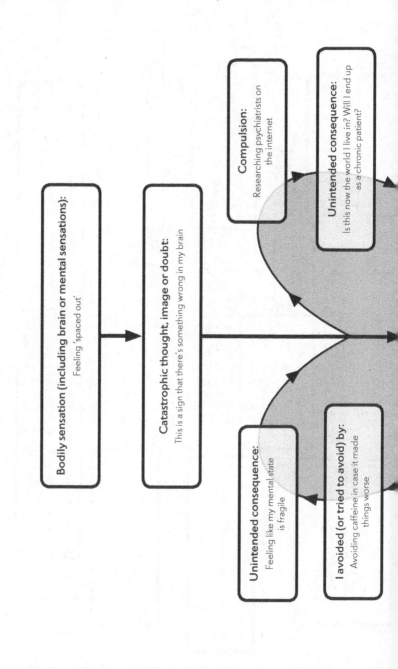

Bodily sensation (including brain or mental sensations):
Feeling 'spaced out'

Catastrophic thought, image or doubt:
This is a sign that there's something wrong in my brain

Compulsion:
Researching psychiatrists on the internet

Unintended consequence:
Is this now the world I live in? Will I end up as a chronic patient?

Unintended consequence:
Feeling like my mental state is fragile

I avoided (or tried to avoid) by:
Avoiding caffeine in case it made things worse

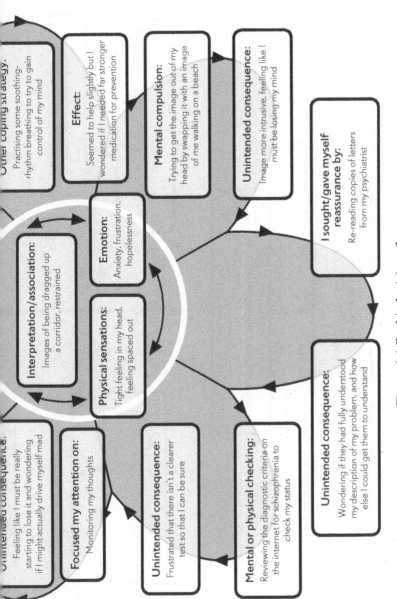

Figure 6.4 Ibrahim's vicious flower

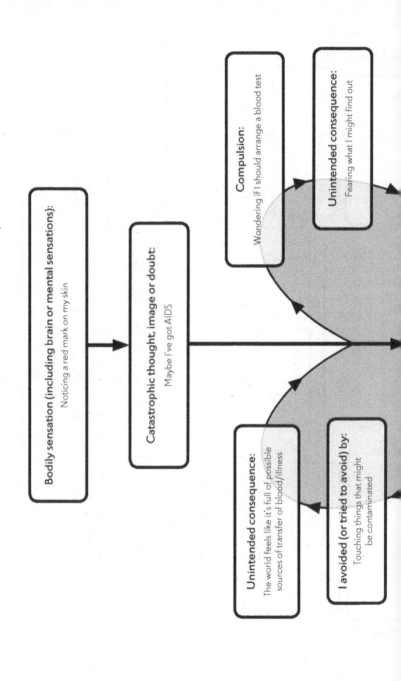

Bodily sensation (including brain or mental sensations):
Noticing a red mark on my skin

Catastrophic thought, image or doubt:
Maybe I've got AIDS

Compulsion:
Wondering if I should arrange a blood test

Unintended consequence:
Fearing what I might find out

Unintended consequence:
The world feels like it's full of possible sources of transfer of blood/illness

I avoided (or tried to avoid) by:
Touching things that might be contaminated

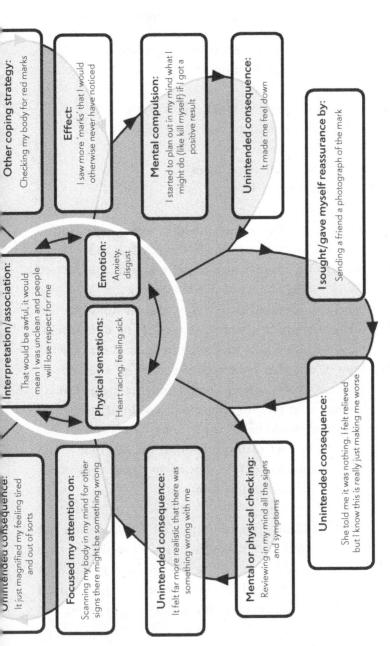

Figure 6.5 Victoria's vicious flower

4. Start putting 'petals' on your flower; identify the 'output' of that interpretation, such as:

    • Compulsions (e.g. bodily checking)
    • Mental compulsions and self-reassurance
    • Avoidance behaviour
    • Changes in attention focus
    • Reassurance seeking

5. The next step is to close the loop with a comment on how that 'output' might be feeding back in and contributing to the maintenance of the problem. Ask yourself 'What is the unintended consequence of . . . . (e.g. checking, avoiding etc.)?' 'How does it make my fear (obsession, anxiety, worry) worse?' 'How does it reinforce the meaning or process at the heart of my anxiety?'

6. Now take a step back and take stock of your flower. Hopefully you will have a better understanding of what's keeping your problem going and can already see where you think would be good places to make a change. For each petal, start to think of ideas on how you could make things different, to start to go *against* your health anxiety, and start to test them out.

Now use the blank diagram on pages 138–9 and draw out your own vicious flower, similar to the examples we have given. You can add or modify this as you learn more about your problem. This will give you your own personalised summary of what is keeping your health anxiety going, and therefore show you what to change to reduce your anxiety and preoccupation.

Theory A versus Theory B

Having got a good understanding of how your health anxiety works, you have a chance to put this into words that help you to define the problem in a way that means trying psychological solutions makes good sense. In the CBT this is called 'Theory B', to be tested out as you tackle your problem, and usually refers to you having a problem with fear, worry and anxiety about being ill. This is contrasted against your 'Theory A', which is your 'old' way of understanding things and which was driving your health anxiety: for example, that the problem is that you must protect yourself from a disease (or pick it up early), or that you've got (or might have) a feared illness that has as yet not been detected.

The way to 'test' theory A versus B is to judge them by their results; which is the most helpful in the long term?

Paul's alternative theories

Paul had been told he was suffering from stress, and it would go away. He didn't find this explanation very helpful. He had then gone to a private doctor for a remote consultation, and they had sent him for a scan. Although this was negative and allayed some of his fears about it being bowel cancer, he was still being told it was 'just stress', meaning that he was

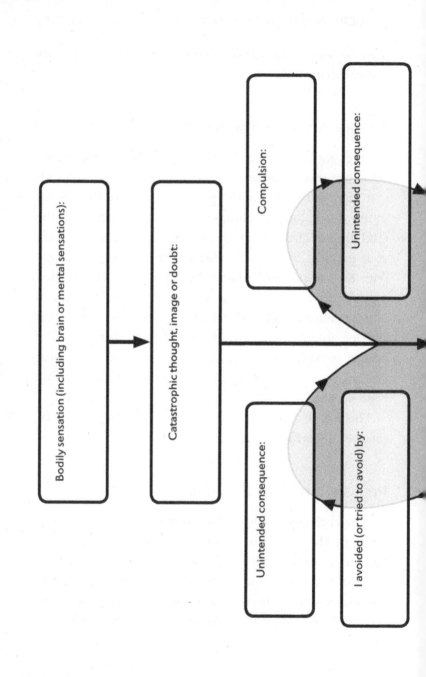

Bodily sensation (including brain or mental sensations):

Catastrophic thought, image or doubt:

Compulsion:

Unintended consequence:

Unintended consequence:

I avoided (or tried to avoid) by:

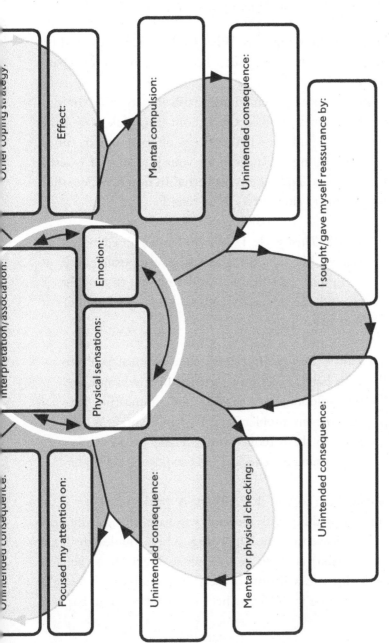

Figure 6.6 Blank vicious flower

imagining his symptoms. What Paul needed was not just to be told what it wasn't, but a better explanation of what it was.

The essence of overcoming health anxiety using the various techniques outlined throughout this book is to gather evidence to find out whether the results of your experiment fit your existing explanation for your problems or whether an alternative explanation fits better. In health anxiety there are two broad alternatives to be tested:

> **Paul's Theory A:** I have an undiagnosed bowel cancer. My solution is to take every possible step to monitor my health, avoid anything that might remind me of death and to keep checking for information.

> **Paul's Theory B:** I have an emotional problem with being excessively worried by my health, and my 'solutions' of checking and monitoring have become my problem and feed my worry. What I need to do is reduce my fear and preoccupation by stopping my checking and avoidance behaviour.

It may seem to you that Theory A works because you are doing something with the tools you have, and you are stopping bad events from happening. The activities are learnt (like a habit) and can be difficult to break. It is therefore likely that you will avoid or escape from unpleasant thoughts and situations in the future because such behaviour has been learnt; it has apparently been successful and given you a 'pay-off'. We are not saying that this is wrong or bad. It just happens because human beings, like other animals, can train themselves to think and behave in a particular way.

In the space overleaf, write under Theory A how you have viewed the problem, and how it has led to your using avoidance and safety behaviours. Then write against Theory B another way of looking at your experience that would enable you to test your alternative.

If you have a health anxiety problem, you will probably have been following Theory A for some time. However, to determine whether Theory B might be a more helpful explanation for your problems, you will have to act *as if* it were correct (even if you don't believe it), at least for a time while you collect the evidence. This may seem rather scary. But think of it like this: if, after, say, three months, you remain unconvinced, you can always go back to Theory A and carry on with your current solutions. You might believe that the risk of being seriously ill through testing out Theory B is too high to take a leap of faith. But if you don't test out Theory B, then we can almost certainly say that your symptoms of health anxiety are likely to progress, and you won't ever know if you can achieve a much better quality of life. If there's nothing there, you can always go back to your theory; but if you don't test out the alternative Theory B, you will be sticking to your own way of coping, causing yourself more distress and limiting your life even more.

Here's some more detail from Paul's example.

Theory A (the one I have been following)	Theory B (the one to be tested)
The problem is: I have an undiagnosed bowel cancer.	The problem is: I have a problem with anxiety and being excessively worried by my health.
If this is true, then I have to act by: I take every possible step to monitor my health, avoid anything that might remind me of death and keep checking for information on early detection of bowel cancer.	If this is true, then I have to act by: What I need to do is reduce my fear and preoccupation by stopping checking and stop monitoring my health. I need to boost my tolerance of uncertainty and keep my attention focused on the outside world.
If this is true, what this says about the future: I'll keep checking and stay anxious, unless I actually get bowel cancer which I don't currently think I could cope with.	If this is true, what this says about the future: If I practise hard, the amount of daily worry I have about bowel cancer will reduce significantly and stop dominating my mind.

Now you try.

Theory A (the one I have been following)	Theory B (the one to be tested)
The problem is:	The problem is:
If this is true, then I have to act by:	If this is true, then I have to act by:
If this is true, what this says about the future:	If this is true, what this says about the future:

7

Reducing worry and dealing with upsetting thoughts

This chapter is about developing a different relationship with your thoughts and doubts so you can treat them as 'just thoughts' and have an alternative explanation for the sensations. Your life will be more rewarding if you can truly accept your thoughts and doubts about your health as just thoughts; whereas trying to 'control' them only makes the worry worse and amplifies your discomfort into pain.

This chapter also contains several practical exercises to help you examine the way you think.

Making friends with uncertainty

Sometimes people who have an anxiety-related condition like health anxiety try and make life feel safer and more predictable as part of an understandable effort to reduce their overall levels of stress. For example, you might try to reduce uncertainty in everyday life by avoiding surprises and always follow the same routines. However, this means you may become less and less flexible and less able to cope with uncertainty, which can ultimately mean more discomfort.

The less you practise tolerating doubts and not knowing, the harder you find it to tolerate them. This will *decrease your confidence in your memory* and you will find it more difficult to know whether something is true or not. This drives your anxiety up and leads you to check, seek reassurance or mentally review past actions. Sometimes the process of checking will turn up ambiguous information and increase your doubts. For example, a woman with health anxiety had doubts about whether she might have cancer. She kept checking on websites and seeking reassurance from friends or going to a doctor. Not surprisingly, she occasionally got conflicting or ambiguous information about whether she could have cancer, and this just fuelled her doubts.

So here are some easy-to-follow rules for when you have an intolerance of uncertainty.

1. Try to set a rule of thumb, 'If it's a doubt, it's health anxiety', to help not engage in such thoughts. Allowing 'just one check' or reassurance may lead to relief in the short term but just strengthens the need for another check and reduces your tolerance of doubt.

2. Don't collect more information that is uncertain or speculative. Thus, one person who was very fearful about the Coronavirus in the first few months, watched and read everything she could find on the

subject. This made her even more confused, with conflicting reports and speculation. This is not surprising with many unknowns (let alone fake news) and lots of conflicting information. In this case it's best to stick to the government advice that tells you *what to do* and to check for any updates on the relevant government site once a week.

3. Sometimes, when intolerance of uncertainty is high, you may freeze and avoid making a decision or not turn up to an event to reduce the feeling of uncertainty. However, not making a decision is also a decision, which also has consequences. Consider the story of the camel in the desert: a camel is deep in a hot and dry desert. She is severely dehydrated and knows that if she doesn't drink very soon, she will surely die. She arrives at a fork in the path. The camel knows that at the end of one way there is fresh, cool, drinking water in a well and at the end of the other there is some dirty water. If she drinks the dirty water, she may get ill for a few days but will very likely survive. However, she does not know which well is which. Because she believes she cannot bear the feeling of not knowing and wants to be 100 per cent certain that she does not drink the dirty water, she is unable to take the risk. That, of course, was the end of the camel as she shrivelled up and died in the desert. What you may learn is that not making a decision (which would mean taking a risk) *is a decision* and has unintended consequences.

4. Find healthy ways of helping your mind gain a sense that all is well and under good enough control, that does not involve your health anxiety. For example, if your life is somewhat chaotic and without any structure, then impose structure to create certainty in your everyday life and what is in your control. Thus, make sure that you structure your day, organise your home, and have a routine of when you get up and have your meals.

    However, you do not want to over-compensate and over-plan with excessive preparation and rigidity in your routine. Thus, once you have some structure in your life, it's important to also consider changing a routine or to experiment with something new to become attuned to the way uncertainty feels. You might start with easy tasks, for example going on a different route to work, trying out different places for leisure and building up to where you go on holiday. There are games of chance that can be played that result in bad luck out of the blue. What you are learning is to tolerate the distress of not knowing. Over time this means you will learn to tolerate the doubts in your health anxiety.

5. Prepare for things that are 100 per cent certain like death and taxes. Have you made your will or discussed your funeral plans? Have you done your tax return? There are also events that are very certain: for example, preparing for an interview that you have been invited for. Wherever possible, practise by

rehearsing for the event by doing a role play (in real life, not in your head). Preparing for an interview by doing a role play is an action and means getting out of your head. This is also relevant for events that are unlikely, but which we still rehearse. For example, we prepare for a fire by doing fire drills, so these routines become ingrained.

6. We have emphasised the importance of not discussing the content of your doubts with yourself or with others (e.g. whether you have, or might get, a particular disease). However, many of your intrusive doubts are just rabbit holes, and the further you go down them the darker and more horrible they are and the harder they are to escape from. Try to identify the chain of events when you first become aware of such doubts, and intervene before the checking, reassurance seeking or self-monitoring. Stick to your path of what's important in your life, tolerating not knowing what is down the rabbit holes and therefore not going down them!

Practising 'detached observation' with your thoughts

Learning to treat your thoughts, including ones you would rather did not enter your mind, as passing events can be a useful way to try and distance yourself from their endless chatter, commentary and rating of yourself. This is a difficult skill, which will take time and practice to master, using several different exercises (described below).

Labelling your thoughts and feelings

An important strategy for dealing with an intrusive thought or feeling is to label it by saying it out loud and writing it down. This can be helpful to stop confusing the thoughts about illness with facts. For example:

> I am **having a thought** that I am ill.
>
> I am **having a memory** of being in hospital as a child.
>
> I'm **having the feeling** of being anxious.
>
> I'm **making a judgement** of myself that I am vulnerable in my health.

As an alternative, some people find it more helpful to distance themselves from such thoughts by labelling them as products of their mind. For example: 'My mind is telling me I am ill.'

EXERCISE 7.1: LABELLING YOUR HABITUAL THOUGHTS

Now try to complete the following for your own habitual pattern of thoughts and feelings:

I am having a thought that (describe)

_____

_____

I am having a thought that (describe)

_____

_____

I am having a feeling of (describe)

_____

_____

I am having memories about (describe)

_____

_____

I am making a rating about (describe)

_____

_____

Labelling your thoughts may feel awkward at first, but with practice it will help you to accept your thoughts or feelings without 'buying into' them. Some people find it helpful to speak their thoughts out loud in a funny voice or in the voice of a cartoon character. Again, this can help you to distance yourself from your thoughts and defuse them from your 'self'.

The aim of all these exercises is to acknowledge the existence of such thoughts and label them for what they are. As you progress, you'll discover that you can experience unpleasant thoughts and feelings and still do what's important for your life, despite their presence. If you keep doing this, they will slowly fade away.

Keeping a record of your thoughts

Try making a list of all your recurrent body image thoughts and feelings, label them for what they are, and add a tick each time they occur. You can use the chart on page 154 and in Appendix 2. Such thoughts are more likely to appear in difficult situations. It can be helpful to monitor them just to see which ones turn up in particular situations and try to 'bully you'. We don't want you to do this repeatedly – just to see what happens over a few days. You will soon start to develop different ways of looking at your thoughts rather than buying into them or paying attention to what your mind is telling you. An example is shown overleaf:

SAMPLE THOUGHT MONITORING CHART

	Mon	Tues	Wed	Thurs	Fri	Sat	Sun
I have thoughts that I'll find out that I'm ill	✓✓ ✓✓ ✓	✓✓ ✓✓	✓✓ ✓✓✓ ✓✓	✓✓ ✓✓			
I have a thought that I'm going to die	✓✓ ✓✓✓	✓✓ ✓✓ ✓✓✓	✓✓ ✓✓✓ ✓✓	✓✓ ✓✓✓			
I have images of myself lying in bed in hospital	✓✓ ✓✓✓ ✓✓	✓✓ ✓✓	✓✓ ✓✓✓ ✓	✓✓ ✓✓			

A blank thought-monitoring chart can be found on the next page, and in Appendix 2, which you can photocopy. Note that the purpose of monitoring your thoughts is not to challenge their content or to control or reduce their frequency – just to acknowledge them, note the thinking error, and to thank your mind for its contribution. If your thoughts are very frequent (and in some people, they may occur a thousand or more times a day) you might find it easier to use a tally counter and transfer the total at the end of each day to your chart. (You can purchase a tally counter over the internet. You will easily find a supplier if you type 'buy tally counter' into an internet search engine.) You can also note the situations in which the thoughts most commonly occur to see if there is a pattern. It would be useful to know if there is such a pattern so that you can predict what thoughts will turn up and ensure that you are better prepared for them.

EXERCISE 7.2: THOUGHT-MONITORING CHART

In the left-hand column note your most common intrusive thoughts and images about your health, and then tick the relevant column (Mon–Sun) each time you have that thought, or add the total from your tally counter.

	Mon	Tues	Wed	Thurs	Fri	Sat	Sun
I have an intrusive thought that							
I have an intrusive thought that							

I have an intrusive thought that	I have an intrusive thought that	I have an intrusive image of	I have an intrusive image of

De-catastrophising 1: Learning to assume less danger

Imagine riding a bicycle that tends to veer to the right when you point the handlebars straight ahead. What would you do to make the bicycle go straight (before you had a chance to fix it)? You would correct for the bias towards the right by steering slightly towards the left.

You can do the same in your mind: so, if you know that you tend to over-assume danger, you can correct your thinking by deliberately assuming your bodily sensations are not necessarily dangerous.

Something that can be very helpful in overcoming catastrophic misinterpretations of bodily or mental sensations is to understand that they may have an alternative explanation – for example, that they are consequences of anxiety. This has two advantages:

1. It's a less scary interpretation of what's going on.
2. It gives you a clear plan for what to change – reducing your anxiety using the techniques we've outlined in this book – rather than checking or seeking reassurance.

There are an enormous number of physical and mental 'outputs' of anxiety, some of which are incredibly powerful. It's therefore easy to see how they could be misinterpreted as a sign of something being wrong, when in fact they are a sign of your body's fight-or-flight anxiety response being in very good working order. The diagram below illustrates some of the more common mental and physical sensations driven by anxiety.

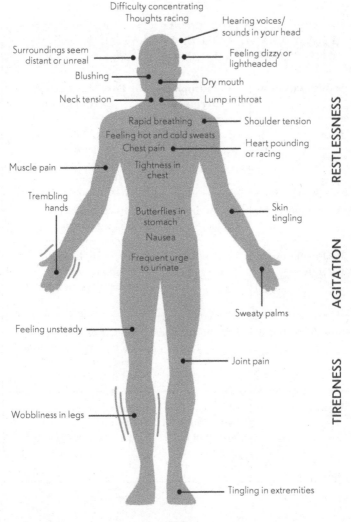

In the following table are some examples of bodily sensations, the kind of catastrophic misinterpretations that are driven by health anxiety, and some alternative explanations.

EXAMPLES OF BODILY SENSATIONS AND POSSIBLE EXPLANATIONS		
Bodily sensation	**Catastrophic misinterpretation**	**Possible alternative explanation**
Joint pain	My bones are wearing out	Some stiffness in joints is completely normal, especially after exercise or inactivity
Ache in my leg	I've got bone cancer	Muscle tension or a strained muscle
Red marks on my skin	I've got skin cancer	A scratch, having knocked against something, an insect bite
Stomach cramps	I've got stomach cancer	Gastric discomfort caused by acid entering your stomach due to stress or anxiety
Heart racing	My overworking heart will be getting worn out	Raised heart rate due to adrenalin caused by stress, anxiety or caffeine

Headache	I've got a brain tumour	Tension created by tightening of the muscles over the skull; may be caused by stress or anxiety, too much caffeine, hangover from too much alcohol or lack of sleep
I can feel a sore patch on my mouth	I've got mouth cancer	A mouth ulcer, a burn from hot food, a scratch from food or toothbrush, having accidentally bitten part of your mouth
Chest pain	I've got a heart problem	Tension in the muscles between your ribs caused by stress or anxiety
Feeling tired all the time	I've got a cancer of the blood cells	Fatigue caused by anxiety, fatigue driven by low mood, being restless and not sleeping well
My surroundings feel distant and unreal	I'm losing touch with reality; I'm going to develop schizophrenia	Being tired, anxiety causing 'derealisation' (a natural protection against stressful events)
Tingling sensations in my hands	I've got multiple sclerosis	Too much oxygen in your blood caused by over-breathing when feeling anxious or stressed

My breasts feel tender	I've got breast cancer	Swelling and tenderness caused by hormonal changes in menstrual cycle, ill-fitting bra, accidental bruising, bruising caused by excessive checking
Can't recall friend's wife's name	I'm getting dementia	Being a bit tired and your mind going a bit blank is just one of those things; you're probably trying too hard to remember
Twitches in my legs	It's a sign of motor neurone disease	Training hard at the gym and not eating all that well, body just recovering

In summary, there is every chance that there is an alternative explanation for your experience of bodily sensations. Consider the following possibilities:

- It's a normal physical sensation that you are focusing upon and is therefore 'amplified' in your awareness, but normally would not be on your mind.
- It's the physical result of your emotions such as anxiety, stress or depression. Again, these can be amplified if you focus upon them.
- It's the result of a minor physical ailment.

You can use the chart below to develop your own, less anxiety-provoking, interpretations of the bodily sensations you tend to worry about.

Remember, not all sensations have a clear explanation, so you might need to take the practical, self-helping decision to assume they are not the product of a disease unless proven otherwise. But this is an uncertain universe and it's important to remember that doubt is normal and it's healthy for our minds to be able to tolerate doubt – so look for probable explanations, not certain ones.

EXERCISE 7.3: ALTERNATIVE EXPLANATIONS

Body sensation	Catastrophic misinterpretation	Possible alternative explanation

Interpretation pie chart

Here's a further strategy to help counter your mind's tendency to jump to a 'worst case' conclusion:

- Identify your belief (e.g. cancerous brain tumour means headache; therefore headache means tumour)
- Rate your belief (0–100 per cent)
- Make a list of all possible causes (for headaches, begin with cancer)
- When the list is complete, divide a pie chart up into rough percentages – *start at the bottom of the list!*
- Re-rate your belief

You can repeat this for past and possible future sensations to give yourself practice in holding in mind that there could be more than one explanation for a bodily or mental sensation. We've put an example below:

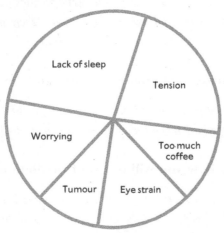

Figure 7.2: Interpretation pie chart

De-catastrophising 2: Conducting a survey to normalise bodily and mental sensations

Another kind of experiment that can help you build confidence that the sensations that you experience, or things you see, in your mind/head/body are normal is to carry out a survey of other people's experience. We've given an illustrated example below.

Describe the problem

I'm worried that when I can't stop my mind racing this is a sign that I might develop schizophrenia, and even though I've seen three doctors I can't be convinced that there's nothing wrong with me.

Identify the prediction you want to test

That other people don't get such strong feelings that they can't stop their mind racing, which means there must be something physically wrong with my mind.

Formulate an alternative prediction

That some people might also have strong mental sensations, especially when they feel anxious or stressed.

Specify how you will test your prediction

I'll conduct a survey of people I know and ask whether they have ever felt their thoughts racing or as if they can't get their mind under control.

Write down the results of your experiment

I spoke to nine people. All could relate to times when they 'feel as if they are going crazy', especially when they feel really stressed and things are getting on top of them.

Analyse the results of your experiment

It seems my mental experience is very normal, especially at times of stress. I suppose that my fear of going mad is leading me to notice these sensations more and to have them more because I'm so stressed by my fear of going mad!

Now try your own experiment.

EXERCISE 7.4: DESCRIBE THE PROBLEM

Identify the prediction you want to test

_____

_____

_____

Formulate an alternative prediction

_____

_____

_____

Specify how you will test your prediction

_____

_____

_____

Write down the results of your experiment

_____

_____

_____

Analyse the results of your experiment

_____

_____

_____

De-catastrophising 3: Not being sure, but treating your problem 'as if' it's anxiety anyway

Trying to be certain about whether your body or mental sensations are a sign of actual or pending disease is part of the problem, not part of the solution. Assuming you've been reassured by a doctor that you are excessively concerned and that, to date, treating your problem as if the problem itself is a disease you are preoccupied with has not helped, your next best step is to try out treating the problem differently. That is, you should try treating your physical sensations and intrusive thoughts and images 'as if' you have a problem with worry about your health (rather than a physical illness).

This means using the approach we outline in this book for several weeks and then stepping back to see the results. If things have improved, then that's further confirmation that your problem is primarily one of worry. If they have not improved, you can reconsider whether you have been targeting your main unhelpful coping strategies and try again. You can of course even ultimately return to treating your problem as if it is a physical illness problem and see if this provides a more effective solution.

Excessive responsibility and blame

Reduce your excessive responsibility that contributes to your fear of missing something important. Remember that the term responsibility refers to the degree of influence you have.

The responsibility pie chart is a great visual tool you can use to help yourself reduce excessive responsibility. You can practise using it on any feared catastrophe (past, present or future) for which you may be taking too much responsibility. If you think 'it is/would be all my fault if I missed something and became seriously ill . . . ' then this exercise is probably for you.

Dividing up your responsibility pie chart

Using the responsibility pie chart effectively has five stages and it's important that you follow them in sequence.

1. Identify the event you fear being responsible or have excessive influence for (e.g. dying of cancer because you did not immediately get checked by your doctor):

_____

_____

2. Write down the degree of responsibility you would currently feel if the event occurred, rating 0–100 per cent:

_____ per cent

3. List all the possible factors which contribute to making the event you fear likely to occur, including yourself:

_____

_____

_____

_____

_____

_____

These factors might include other moments in the future when you discuss your health with a doctor, the observations your friends, family or colleagues might make about your health, the care you receive, the state of medical science, other aspects of your health, your genes and so on.

4. Divide up your responsibility pie chart

Using the circle to represent 100 per cent, roughly divide the pie amongst the factors you've listed above. Be sure to put yourself in last.

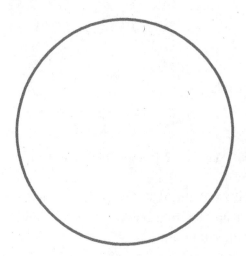

5. Re-rate your estimation of your responsibility for your feared event 0–100 per cent:

_____ per cent

It's worth noting that your responsibility pie chart isn't intended to be a 100 per cent accurate, scientific-type exercise but is mainly to help your mind develop a less black-or-white view of responsibility.

An example is provided.

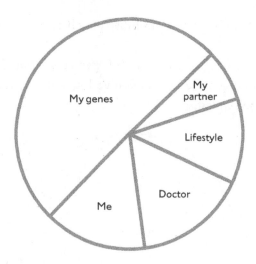

Figure 7.3 Responsibility pie chart

The feared outcome that I am preoccupied with: that I might die painfully from bowel cancer as a result of missing an important symptom.

Possible contributing factors:

- My genes
- Lifestyle factors
- My partner not noticing changes
- My doctor not detecting the problem and his treatment

- Me missing something because I reduce my checking and vigilance

Watching your thoughts pass by

You have gathered by now that what we want you to develop is a sense of distance from your thoughts and feelings. This means not buying into them but being aware of them as a passive observer.

This is best illustrated by closing your eyes and recalling, say, a bowl of fruit, then watching it without influencing it in any way. It's OK if your attention strays away from the orange or if the image changes (for example, the orange falls off the top of the bowl). You should merely be aware of the changing content of your attention without influencing the content in any way. This may not be easy at first, but it's worth persevering. The technique of distancing your thoughts can also be used simply to notice your intrusive thoughts and not to engage with them.

Another analogy for watching your thoughts is to imagine them as cars passing on a road. When you are anxious, you might focus on particular 'cars' that tell you that you have cancer. You cope either by trying to stop the cars or by pushing them to one side (if you're not in danger of being run over, that is!). Alternatively, you may try to flag the car down, get into the driving seat and try to park it (that is, analyse the idea and sort it out until you feel 'right'). Of course, there is often no room to park the car, and as soon as you have parked one car, another one comes along.

An exercise in distancing

In this exercise, you will need to get into a relaxed position and just observe the flow of your thoughts, one after another, without trying to work out their meaning or their relationship to one another. You are practising an attitude of acceptance of your experience.

Imagine for the moment sitting next to a stream. As you gaze at the stream, you notice several leaves on the surface of the water. Keep looking at the leaves and watch them drift slowly downstream. When thoughts come, put each one on a leaf and notice each leaf as it comes closer to you. Then watch it slowly moving away from you, eventually drifting out of sight. Return to looking at the stream, waiting for the next leaf to float by with a new thought. If one comes along, again, watch it come closer to you and then let it drift out of sight. Allow yourself to have thoughts and imagine them floating by like leaves down a stream. Notice now that you are the stream. You hold all the water, all the fish and debris and leaves. You need not interfere with anything in the stream – just let them all flow. Then, when you are ready, gradually widen your attention to take in the sounds around you. Slowly open your eyes and get back to life.

Distancing yourself from your thoughts means being on the pavement, acknowledging the cars and the traffic but just noticing them and then walking along the pavement and focusing your attention on other parts of the environment (such as talking to the person beside you and noticing other people passing you and the sights and smells of the flowers on the verge). You can still 'play in the park' and do what is important to you despite the thoughts. In other words, such thoughts have no more meaning than passing traffic – they are 'just' thoughts and are part of the rich tapestry of human existence. You can't get rid of them. It's just the same as when you are in a city and there is always some slight traffic noise in the background, and you learn to live with it. Notice these thoughts and feelings and acknowledge their presence, then get on with your life.

Worry as a process

One way of looking at health anxiety is to think of it as something that you *do* rather than something that you *suffer from*. Your natural question in response might well be 'why would I do this to myself?!' One of the dilemmas in overcoming health anxiety can be that you might, to some extent at least, think it is perfectly reasonable to worry about your health. This idea alone could contribute to years of needless distress, preoccupation and interference in your life. Let's be clear: an appropriate degree of concern and sensible health behaviours is a very long way from the kind of excessive worry that health anxiety involves.

We understand how difficult it is to stop worrying and how habitual it may be. We understand how powerful your thoughts can be when they are pulled by emotions. However, we are now going to show you ways in which you can begin to escape the power of worrying. The first step in understanding worrying is to analyse the process. We are going to show you how to understand when you worry, and what happens when you worry, to work out what keeps it going. Your eventual goal will be to stop engaging in the content of your worries.

If your worrying helps you to achieve what you want (and please write to us with some examples), then you can stop at this chapter! If, however, it makes you feel worse or causes you to become inactive or to do something else that is unhelpful, then read on. If you are not sure whether your worrying is helpful, keep a record of its frequency over the next few days, using the chart on page 176, and complete the analysis. If you are still not sure, try to alternate a period (e.g. one day) of worrying extra hard with equal periods of not worrying at all and note the effect on your mood and what you avoid.

Cost-benefit analysis

To help say good riddance to worrying about your health it can be useful to do a 'cost-benefit' analysis on worry. In doing so you can consider the advantages and disadvantages of worrying about your health. When you do this exercise, consider the following:

- What are the advantages and disadvantages to **yourself** of worrying?
- What are the advantages and disadvantages **to other people** of worrying?
- What are the advantages and disadvantages of worrying **in the short term**?

- What are the advantages and disadvantages of worrying **in the long term**?

Here's an example below:

Benefits of worrying about my health	Costs of worrying about my health
I feel like I'm not just taking my health for granted. I'm less likely to miss something important. It might mean I'm less likely to let cancer get the better of me. Even if I do get ill, maybe I'll feel like I've done all I can. I'm trying to prevent the people I care about from dealing with the pain of me being ill and dying too soon.	I feel a lot of anxiety and feel guilty when I'm not worrying. All this extra stress can't be good for me. While I worry so much about cancer I might not be paying attention to other aspects of my health. No matter how careful I am, it never feels like I'm doing enough to avoid getting ill. My worrying excessively really gets on the nerves of the people who care about me I feel more tired and with less headspace for other important things in life than I would if I worried less.

Next consider the pros and cons of reducing your worry about your health (to yourself and others).

EXERCISE 7.5: COST-BENEFIT ANALYSIS: REDUCING WORRY	
Costs of reducing my worry about my health	**Benefits of reducing my worry about my health**

Motivations to worry

If you think it's reasonable to worry, then it's very under-standable that this worrying is something that you *do*. Furthermore, you are not in a strong position to develop the skills to overcome it. Having some *positive* beliefs about worry is extremely common, but the problem is sometimes compounded by the fact that people will then also worry that anxiety and worry *itself* might cause them harm. Being aware of how these thoughts might be steering you directly into health anxiety and considering whether these beliefs really are worth listening to will help you to overcome the problem.

Here are some examples of the positive beliefs and motiv-ations that people with health anxiety have about worrying and being preoccupied about their health:

- If I don't worry about my health, I might miss some-thing important.
- If I don't worry about my health, I might regret not being careful enough if I become ill.
- Worrying means I don't have to think about the bad things that are happening in my life now.
- Thoughts about this illness must be on my mind for a reason; ignoring them is irresponsible.
- Ignoring thoughts about illness is tempting fate.
- If I don't worry, I might neglect my health and become really unhealthy.
- Worrying will give me some hope of being mentally prepared for the worst.
- Because my feared illness is so awful it would be silly and irresponsible not to worry about it.

- Something like my health is so important that being certain everything is fine is the only way I could ever stop worrying.
- If a health professional has given me important information about my health, I should remind myself of it regularly so that I don't forget it.

EXERCISE 7.6: POSITIVE BELIEFS ABOUT WORRY

List your own positive beliefs about the process of worrying over your health. What are your most important beliefs that motivate you to worry about your health?

1 _____

_____

2 _____

_____

3 _____

_____

4 _____

_____

Negative beliefs about worry

It's very understandable for positive beliefs to promote worrying and increase your tendency to focus on your body and to carry out safety-seeking behaviours such as checking, seeking medical investigations and reassurance-seeking. Equally you may have several negative beliefs about worrying that make you anxious. Here are some examples of the *negative* beliefs and motivations that people with health anxiety give about worrying about their health:

- If I worry too much, then I might push my mind over the edge into a serious mental illness.
- If I worry then I won't be able to think straight and rationally.
- All this worry might be putting too much strain on my heart.
- I can't concentrate and I'll end up doing worse at work/school, etc.
- I feel as if I'm losing my mind.
- I can't be the kind of friend/partner/parent etc. that I want to be because I can't cope with thinking about other things.
- I'm sure all this stress is making me more prone to illness/cancer.
- Because I'm so worried all the time people won't take me seriously.

Again, it's easy to see how these thoughts may further compound the problem. The danger is that many people who suffer from health anxiety try to deal with the negative aspects of worrying by simply trying harder to eliminate the uncertainties that they worry about. The downside is that this usually makes their worry worse, forming a vicious cycle.

EXERCISE 7.7: NEGATIVE BELIEFS ABOUT WORRY

What are your most important negative beliefs about the process of worrying? For example, 'Too much worrying will make me more stressed and make me ill.'

1 _____

_____

2 _____

_____

3 _____

_____

4 _____

_____

Now that you are more aware of the thoughts that influence your worrying, you can begin to be less influenced by them and, we hope, ultimately come to detach from and ignore them.

Now reconsider your beliefs about worrying about your health. Consider each of your positive and negative beliefs you have listed above. The type of questions to ask yourself are:

- Does this belief about worrying help me to overcome my health anxiety?
- Does my belief help me to follow the directions in life that I want to follow? What alternative actions can I take?
- While I hold this belief about my worrying, do I become more preoccupied and act in ways that are unhelpful?
- Would I teach these attitudes about worrying about health to a child? If not, why not?

In the following exercise write down some alternative beliefs about worry that will help you develop a more appropriate level of concern about your health and enable you to free yourself from health anxiety. Here is an example:

EXERCISE 7.8: COMPARING BELIEFS ABOUT WORRY

Example:

Positive belief about worry: 'Worrying mentally prepares me for the worst.'

Alternative belief about worry: 'In reality I can only deal with being diagnosed with a serious illness if and when it happens. Worry just makes me feel more anxious and interferes in my ability do things that are important now.'

Alternative actions: 'I can stop avoiding the situations I fear and just experience the intrusive thoughts and images when they are triggered without trying to solve them as current threats.'

Now consider your own beliefs:

Positive/negative belief:

_____

_____

_____

Alternative belief:

_____

_____

_____

Alternative actions:

_____

_____

_____

Now that you have a stronger commitment to overcoming your tendency to worry, we hope that you will:

- try treating your problem 'as if' it is a worry problem;
- spot when you are engaging in the process of worrying excessively about your health;
- bring the focus of your mind back on to the outside world in the here and now;
- decide to deal with being mentally or physically ill or dying if/when it happens (we'll all eventually die somehow!);
- take a reasonable degree of care of your physical and mental health and get on with what's important to you in your life in the meantime.

Being healthy in the way you access healthcare

To put your mind at rest you may be seeking frequent reassurance from your family doctor or going direct to various specialists. Doctors generally want to help you and will order a new test in the hope that it will reassure you and exclude anything serious.

Quite often, in listening to a patient's history, a doctor begins to form a diagnosis even before any examination. The processes of examining you and receiving a positive test result just confirms what the doctor already knew or gives the doctor the location of the problem. If an examination or a test is found to be negative, then it will reassure a patient and that is the end of the matter. However, getting reassurance from a doctor or receiving a negative test result does not usually help someone with health anxiety in the long term. This is because reassurance only works in the short term. It doesn't take long before a doubt pops into your mind about what the doctor might have missed.

Even before you get the results, you may be thinking that having a test must mean that the doctor thinks there is something wrong with you. As we have already discussed, doctors normally operate like this, but they have a different motivation from someone with health anxiety – they are examining you or ordering a test to reassure you. Or they may give you an unnecessary medication to reduce your symptoms. In other words, they are buying into your anxiety because they don't want to see you suffer. The same sequence of events can take place if you see an alternative practitioner. He or she may provide a credible explanation (e.g. you have an allergy or your meridians are wrong) and then prescribe a remedy. Alternative practitioners are often popular because they have more time than your family doctor to listen to you. They may be very compassionate and make you feel understood.

The results of an examination or a test or a new remedy may be helpful initially. Sometimes the symptom goes away, usually because body sensations are self-limiting and go away by themselves. But then the doubts return. Sometimes the worry moves on to a different area of the body, with a new symptom. Sometimes the doubts about the original test persist. In general, the more times you check something, the more that checking increases your doubt. Even if a test is negative the doubt might be 'What if it's something else the doctor has missed?', 'What if the laboratory made a mistake?', 'What if the test doesn't pick up what I've got?'

Sometimes posting a message on the internet can make things worse because other well-meaning individuals will suggest tests that you need and what to say to your doctor. There are a number of possible disadvantages and unintended consequences from frequently seeking reassurance from your doctors.

a) The more tests you have, the more likely you are to have a false positive. This is a result that suggests something positive, but which is a mistake. This usually leads to more false leads and unnecessary tests to exclude the positive result. This in turn increases your doubts and worries.

b) Some doctors use medical terms that sound impressive but are fairly meaningless or descriptions of a normal variation in everyone. For example, androgenic alopecia simply means normal male pattern baldness. Premature atrial contractions of the heart are usually perfectly normal or related to caffeine or exercise. Using medical terminology feeds your doubts by making a condition sound pathological when it's a quite normal variation.

c) Some tests are painful or have a risk of causing an illness. We have seen people with chest pain caused by anxiety have an X-ray that involves catheterisation of the cardiac vessels. This is an important investigation if you have heart disease since it tells a surgeon exactly where to operate – however, there is a small risk it could cause a heart attack. This is a risk worth taking if it is to save your life in an operation, but it is not an investigation to reassure someone they do not have heart disease.

d) Most doctors are caring and do not want you to suffer. If you are seeking help privately, less scrupulous doctors might cotton on to your fears and will provide you with as much reassurance and tests as you want, partly for a financial motive. Thus, in some countries, like the United States, there are many more investigations than in the United Kingdom, but US citizens are not healthier. Even in a public service, some doctors will order as many tests as you want in a genuine desire to reassure you. Doctors may also be acting defensively and be driven more by a fear of litigation and a concern not to miss anything important. In summary, some doctors may be more anxious and cannot tolerate uncertainty – so they order more tests so they can feel less anxious even if other doctors might consider such tests to be unnecessary.

e) Over time, a doctor might develop a jaundiced view of your worries and privately label you as a hypochondriac. They might not listen to you seriously when you really do have a problem. We don't think this happens very often but it's very understandable if you have been complaining of various symptoms for many years, none of which has been serious.

How to get the most from your doctor

1. It is important to maintain a good relationship with your family doctor. Try to use one doctor whom you trust and who understands your history of health anxiety – don't doctor shop. We appreciate that this is becoming more difficult in many group practices. This includes seeking reassurance from friends who are doctors or alternative health practitioners.

2. Ask your doctor to treat you like any other patient. If the doctor is concerned about a symptom and wants to exclude something serious then he will order a test. He or she should not order a test with the aim of reassuring you – because this does not help your mental health. Nearly all diagnoses can be made from examining your

history. Sometimes a physical examination or test may add some extra information or confirm a doctor's diagnosis, but it rarely picks up anything new. Equally, it is important not to refer to yet another medical specialist – it's more important to refer you to a cognitive behaviour therapist who can follow a protocol for treating health anxiety.

3. Only you can experience your pain or symptom. No one else can know what you feel. You can't 'imagine' your pain, and if a doctor tells you that you are just imagining things, then it's probably better to find one who can better understand health anxiety. It's true that some of the ways you cope may be aggravating your symptoms, for example repeatedly pressing on a body part to check for lumps might make you sore and swollen.

4. Try to choose a doctor who can understand your distress but gives you relevant information about the cause of your symptoms (e.g. 'the chest pain that you experience is caused by tension from the muscles in your chest wall') and even demonstrate to you how the symptoms come about. What is less helpful is bland reassurance that you have not got what you fear you've got or repetition of the same information. So, it's important to try to train your doctor to explain to you what your symptoms are, not what they are not.

5. When you have persistent symptoms, it may be difficult for you and your doctor to know when to stop having investigations. You may want to stop having tests when you feel 'comfortable' or it feels 'right'. In other words,

not only do you want the test result to be negative, but you also want them to change the way you feel. Unfortunately, negative test results don't always lead you to feel comfortable and can be an unhelpful way of trying to change the way you feel.

It is acceptable medical practice to wait and see what happens (i.e. to ask you to come back in three months' time) for many unexplained or persistent symptoms when the history does not suggest anything serious. If you have had a relevant investigation, then a new test is very unlikely to reveal anything new. Some people find that continuing appointments with their doctor and the provision of various remedies (such as bandages, lotions, vitamins, heat pads, massage) helps to provide tangible evidence of their doctor's understanding and acknowledgement of one's own suffering. In general, we think it is better to focus your energy on doing things in life despite your symptoms and not to medicalise your symptoms – and to really commit yourself to treating them as a health anxiety problem.

One good option is to sign up to a psychological therapy (CBT) for three months, and if, after that period, your symptoms persist, you can always go back to your doctor and ask him or her to think again and obtain another opinion. When we say commit yourself, this will mean consistently dropping all your avoidance and checking behaviours and acting as if you have a problem of health anxiety (even if you aren't 100 per cent convinced). It will mean not seeking reassurance for your symptom or researching it more on the internet. It means not mentally planning your next investigation or doctor to visit. It also means no longer reassuring yourself or trying to solve your mental health problem as a physical problem.

6. If you have a medical problem like diabetes, it will be more difficult for the doctor to sort out what should be investigated and what may be related to your health anxiety. Again, your doctor should treat you like any other patient with the same medical problem and only investigate a symptom if he or she wants to and not because you want to be reassured.

Make a note here of any changes you think you should make in the way you use healthcare. Remember, if you have a 'care-avoiding' type of health anxiety, this might mean seeing your doctor more rather than less.

_____

_____

_____

_____

_____

_____

_____

Practise compassion

You may have heard of a newer form of CBT called compassion-focused therapy. At the time of writing, there is no evidence CFT *by itself* can treat health anxiety. However, we think this holds the most promise as an extra module for specialist treatment of severe health anxiety.

As we've already discussed, having health anxiety is one of several things that can go awry with our tricky human brain. We have this complex lump of grey matter in our heads and no User Manual to go with it. You didn't design your brain or your emotional system, you were given it. We are designed for survival rather than happiness. Our ancestors probably survived to pass on their genes owing to their tendency to take the position of 'better safe than sorry'. Health anxiety uses this bias to its advantage.

Compassion is defined as the process of showing sensitivity to the suffering of your 'self' and others and having a deep commitment to trying to relieve it. This is done by developing empathy, sympathy and kindness, by being non-judgemental and by tolerating distress and approaching difficulties with courage. We hope we have incorporated many of these qualities throughout this book and that you use them in the process of testing out your fears and being compassionate to that part of your 'self' that is struggling with your health anxiety. CFT is rooted in evolutionary psychology and an understanding of the tricky relationship between your 'old' brain and the 'new' brain. There is evidence that stimulating your compassion can regulate your threat system and anxiety. Being motivated to practise compassion towards your 'self' requires a deep commit-ment. It might be especially helpful in those who struggle with CBT as they are very self-critical and display marked shame about having health anxiety. For those who want to learn about compassion-focused approaches we recommend Mary Welford's *The Compassionate Mind Approach to Building Self-confidence* and *The Compassionate Mind Workbook* by Chris Irons and Elaine Beaumont, or (from the originator of the approach) Paul Gilbert's *The Compassionate Mind*.

Validate your feelings

Part of practising self-compassion is to show a warmth and understanding towards your emotions. It can be helpful to write a compassionate letter to yourself to summarise the situation in which you find yourself.

Dear me,

I understand that you feel very anxious about fail-ing to prevent or cause harm.

I know that as a human being I have a tricky brain. It is designed to keep me safe and not to be happy. I was born with certain genes and I was shaped during my childhood in ways that I had no choice over. I have been avoiding situations and doing compulsions for some time and so it has become like a habit. So, when the threat system in me says I am in danger, I try to reach out and seek emotional support and connect with others. I understand this is tough and it's going to take a bit of time to reverse a pattern of thinking and behaving that's been with me for many years. I am going to do all I can to have the courage to do things. This means I will feel anxious, but I can bear this. I will keep testing out my prediction and see if my problem is one of fear rather than one of harm coming to my loved ones. We can get through this together.

With love,

Me

8

Reducing anxiety by facing your fears

Very likely, you intuitively know that the best way to overcome a fear is to face it. It's the main treatment for phobias
such as fear of spiders, heights or snakes. In the case of health
anxiety, the 'fear' is not just of a situation or activity, but
also of the thoughts, images, doubts and sensations that it
triggers. This chapter is about building a plan to tackle your
fears head-on. Psychologists call the therapeutic use of facing your fears *exposure*. When it is combined with resisting
rituals, such as checking and reassurance-seeking, it is called
exposure and response prevention (ERP, for short). This process
can also include a 'behavioural experiment' to test out a prediction that you make about what you experience, especially
on how your problem works. One of your predictions might
be how severe the distress is going to be or how long it might
go on for at the end of exposure. Or it may be helpful to test
whether the result of the experiment bests fits Theory A or
Theory B. A quick reminder on Theory A versus B below:

Theory A (the one that you are following) is that you
have a physical illness or that the problem is that you don't

have clear enough information on whether you have a condition or not. Theory B is that you have a problem with being excessively worried and not tolerating doubts about your health. This predicts that, by following Theory A, you are increasing your worry and distress about your health. When you act as if Theory B is right, then your worry and distress about your health will decrease.

One way of looking at health anxiety is to understand it as a problem of having become intolerant of doubts about your health. Thus, you can view facing your fears and deliberately provoking those doubts as a way of giving yourself an opportunity to practise building up your degree of tolerance of kinds of uncertainty.

Anxiety is nothing to be afraid of

It's quite common in health anxiety to fear that too much anxiety can be harmful. But remember that anxiety, though uncomfortable, will not damage you – it's a natural process evolved over millions of years. If you approach your fears too gradually, you'll only reinforce the idea that anxiety is potentially harmful.

Exposure and behavioural experiments

As we've seen earlier, exposure is the process of facing your fears for therapeutic reasons and a behavioural experiment is aimed at gathering evidence. By acting as if Theory B is true, you will learn that you can tolerate your anxiety *provided* you are not doing something to seek safety (such as reassuring yourself or checking your body) and are always testing out your expectations and seeing if Theory B fits with the evidence.

Here's some of the key components of effectively facing your fears:

- Planning to face your fears deliberately and repeatedly (i.e. it's not the same as your anxiety being triggered out of the blue).
- Not responding to them with checking, reassurance or other safety-seeking behaviours.
- You need to practise at a high enough level of anxiety and for long enough to build up your tolerance.
- This recognises that the anxiety may not reduce in a particular session of exposure, but it gets easier when you repeat it again and again.

Courage

Being *willing* to experience feelings of anxiety is crucial. We don't want you to act as if you are on a roller coaster, clinging onto the handrail for dear life, gritting your teeth and desperately waiting for it to be over. We want you to develop the courage to approach uncomfortable thoughts, feelings and memories. Of course, courage does not just come out of the blue; when you approach difficult situations, you will feel anxious. You cannot have courage without feeling anxious.

'Graded' exposure

Many people believe that with exposure, you must do it *gradually*. They might think that too much anxiety can be harmful. This is not true. Yes, exposure is often done in a graded manner, with a series of steps (called a 'hierarchy'), so that you face your less intimidating fears first and confront the most difficult last. But grading your exposure is just a means to an end, and new research suggests that jumping around the hierarchy in different situations is more effective than slavishly sticking to doing easy things then moving up the hierarchy in a very gradual way, e.g. doing something easy then something very slightly more difficult, and so on, which could take years. Remember these key points about anxiety:

- Feeling anxiety or fear, though uncomfortable, will not harm you.
- If you approach your fears too gradually, you'll only reinforce the idea that anxiety is potentially harmful or should be avoided because it is too uncomfortable.
- The rationale is learning to *tolerate* anxiety so elevated fear should be maintained and this does not usually occur at the lower levels of an anxiety hierarchy. The aim is *not* to wait until the fear reduces. This is an older view of exposure by 'habituation' but has been updated as anxiety does not always reduce within an exposure session, yet people still benefit from the exposure.

- In dealing with health anxiety, you have to turn your thinking 'upside down': the more you try to avoid anxiety or uncertainty in the short term, the more of it you're likely to have in the long term.
- Interpreting your anxiety as a natural reaction – your mind and body trying to keep you safe – will help you to feel better.

With any exposure, it really is crucial that you stick with the anxiety; otherwise, you run the risk of reinforcing the idea that anxiety is harmful. If the anxiety is persisting for longer than two hours, then you may be performing a subtle safety behaviour or not fully engaging in the exposure, and it might be best to seek professional help to make progress.

One way of remembering what exposure and response prevention means, is the 'FEAR' acronym: Face Everything And Recover.

> **F**ace
> **E**verything
> **A**nd
> **R**ecover

Here are the key steps of exposure and response prevention

1. *Develop a list of planned exposure tasks*

    A list of tasks is the basis of a step-by-step plan that you can carry out to do exposure. Ensure you understand the rationale and purpose of the exposure. Make a list of your tasks for exposure – the things you tend to avoid because they activate your fears. These may be activities, situations, substances, people, words, sounds, objects or ideas – the range will depend on your fear. Decide on when you will do the task, where you will do it, what resources you will need and how it can be repeated in different contexts. Remember we mainly want anti-health anxiety tasks which involve going 'over the top' and doing things that some people will consider 'abnormal'. Choose tasks which relate to what you avoid, what is driven by your values, and what involves over-learning (these are the anti-health anxiety tasks).

Try to group the activities you fear or avoid into different themes (e.g. COVID-19, motor neurone disease) and, within the themes, try to put them in order of how much distress you would feel if you did the exposure task. You can measure the amount of distress by using a rating scale of 'SUDs'. SUD stands for Subjective Units of Distress, whereby 0 is no distress at all and 100 is overwhelming distress. In the second column of Exercise 8.1 on page 205, give each trigger a rating according to how much distress you'd expect to feel if you experienced that trigger and didn't perform a compulsion. For example, you may rate looking at images related to your feared disease as 65 out of 100. Another individual with health anxiety might rate watching a video about a hospice 99 SUDs out of 100, and so on. Remember to grade them roughly into Low, Moderate or High levels of anticipated distress and *when you do the exposure, jump around the different levels rather than slavishly sticking to the easier ones.*

Here are some examples of exposure tasks for health anxiety:

- Write out and repeatedly read over a description of your feared event, such as sitting in the doctor's office being told that you are seriously ill and have only a few months to live. Write this out as if you were experiencing it in the 'here and now'.
- Put together a scrap book or collage of anxiety-provoking headlines from newspapers and magazines about your health concern. Look at this several times a day until it bores you.
- Visit a graveyard to trigger the thoughts and feelings you have about death.
- Cut and paste the more anxiety-provoking words you can find on websites. It is crucial, however, that you edit out any of the reassuring information. This is facing your fears – not a reassurance session.
- Visit a hospital or accident and emergency department.
- Visit or volunteer at a hospice.
- Visit or volunteer at a health-related charity shop.
- Listen to podcasts or videos about your feared illness.
- Read books of peoples' accounts of being terminally ill.
- Make a will.

Exposure in imagination

Sometimes it is not possible to do an exposure task in real life (e.g. tasks related to your worst fears of dying from cancer). However, you can still create a narrative in your imagination. It's probably helpful to get guidance from a professional on what might be helpful.

If you use imaginal exposure:

a) Write it out or record it in the first person, e.g. 'I am . . . '

b) Try to use as many different senses as possible, e.g. what you saw, what you heard, what you smelled and what was going through your mind. Include the scariest parts, e.g. 'My children were devastated after me dying of cancer'. Sometimes it can be help-ful to write out the words and plaster them all over your walls.

Giving intrusive thoughts a concrete form

For exposure tasks involving some intrusive thoughts and images, it is often helpful to make them as concrete and comical as possible. Ways of doing this might include the following:

- if an intrusive image is disturbing you, try to draw or paint or construct it (e.g. someone with an intrusive image of dying on a cancer ward could make a collage of pictures from the internet)

2. Deliberately face your fears

The critical point about a hierarchy of exposure is that you do not stick slavishly to starting at the bottom and working your way up. It is more effective to jump around and consistently focus on trying to tackle the more difficult tasks.

- Set a particular time frame, which you then keep to, like a set of instructions.
- Decide which targets you will take from the hierarchy and, for each, deliberately face your fear.
- Choose targets that are challenging but not overwhelming.
- Power through the easier targets if they are not sufficiently anxiety-provoking. You may need to ask a friend to come up with suitable tasks that are more challenging.
- The hierarchy must include things that you wouldn't normally do or that seem bizarre (these are the anti-health anxiety tasks).
- Sometimes, *imagining* your worst fears can be the most appropriate step or exposure. However, imagined exposure is, in general, not as potent as doing exposure in real life. If practical, it is best to follow it up with actual situations or activities that are associated with the fear.

We have included a table for you to complete on page 205. (There is another blank copy in Appendix 2). Remember, it's helpful to think of exposure as a way of testing out your Theory B – your theory that you have a problem of fear, worry or preoccupation. Facing your fears is a way of treating the problem 'as if' it's Theory B.

Example exposure list:	
Planned exposure (object, word, place, person, situation, substance)	**Anticipated distress 0–100 SUDs (Subjective Units of Distress)**
Visiting an oncology ward	95
Reading my own written account of my doctor telling me I've got cancer and I could have caught it earlier	90
Drawing a picture of myself being buried underground, life going on without me, I've been replaced, and nobody seems to miss me	80

Reading a book about someone dying of cancer	75
Watching a medical documentary about cancer	75
Watching a medical drama episode about cancer	60
Making a page of 'trigger' words and pictures	40
Looking at a page of 'trigger' words	30

Exercise 8.1: Exposure task list

Planned exposure (object, word, place, person, situation, substance)	Anticipated distress 0–100 SUDs (Subjective Unit of Distress)

3. Make sure the exposure is challenging enough

Always make sure that your exposure is challenging and potent, both in respect of the trigger you are facing and the time you expose yourself to it. Face your fear for long enough for you to *tolerate* the anxiety or disgust. Exposures do not *have to be* long, and sometimes quite a short exposure time may be effective. What is more important is that there is change in the level of anxiety or confirmation of alternative understanding of the problem (Theory B). This means that there is sufficient time to be surprised and mess up Theory A.

- When you look at images related to your feared illness, you might feel for example a rating of 85 SUDs; this is understandable. You are learning to tolerate the anxiety and to test out your expectations – this means finding out whether your experiences best fit with Theory B. The longer you stick with it the more you are learning that you can tolerate it and you do not for example lose control.

- Try to tackle the processes in health anxiety, such as the effect of choosing to live with uncertainty for the benefit of your overall health. Don't wait for the anxiety to subside when you carry out each exposure – it will not necessarily do so, and this is good because you are learning to tolerate the anxiety. Your level of anxiety will tend to diminish each time you repeat the exposure.

4. *Make the exposure frequent enough*

- Repeat the exposure as often as possible in different situations.
- Daily exposure is an absolute minimum until the anxiety lessens in the same or similar situations.
- Leaving long gaps between exposure means fears will return.
- You can never do too much exposure: aim for several times a day in different activities and situations.
- Changes in anxiety within an exposure session are not so important – you want to have elevated fears *within* the session so that it gets easier *between* each task. Always think about how you can incorporate exposure into your everyday life so that it is easier to carry it out on several occasions every day.
- Try to practise your exposure tasks across different contexts (e.g. when alone, in unfamiliar places, at different times).

5. *Avoid using anxiety-reducing strategies or safety-seeking behaviours*

Do the exposure without distraction, drugs, alcohol, compulsions or other safety-seeking behaviours such as saying a comforting phrase to yourself or obtaining reassurance. The key is to understand the function of these activities – to reduce anxiety. If you break up the exposure this will interfere in your ability to test out your fears. Remember to act according to your values or your best interests (Theory B), not according to how you feel and wanting to escape (Theory A). It may be helpful *to act as if* you are not afraid even if you feel frightened.

It's helpful to 'engage fully' with the exposure compassionately, which means:

- using courage to approach the difficult situations that are anxiety provoking
- noticing the catastrophic thoughts and images
- practising being understanding and sympathetic towards yourself
- encouraging yourself in a soothing kind tone
- helpfully labelling the emotion, i.e. 'OK, these are my feelings of anxiety with some anger creeping in.'
- tolerating your feelings of anxiety by just doing the exposure without condemning, judging, blaming or pitying yourself or biting your tongue until you get through it. This is especially important if your exposure is reactivating an old memory which has been traumatic for you. The goal is just to fully accept the memory with the anxiety: don't engage with any of the intrusive thoughts or images. 'Accept' does not mean resigning yourself to being bad or that your anxiety will go on for ever, it just means not judging and not fighting it.
- not using alcohol or 'as required' medication such as alprazolam to dampen your anxiety as this will become a safety behaviour

If you're not sure about whether what you're doing is a safety-seeking behaviour, ask yourself what the intention of the behaviour is. If the objective is to reduce the risk of harm or to make you feel less anxious, then it is a safety-seeking behaviour and will reinforce your beliefs about being able to prevent harm. If the aim is to help you achieve your task so you can move on and do something more challenging without the behaviour, then this is enhancing your exposure and is a means towards an end.

6. *Monitor your exposure tasks*

Monitor your exposure regularly, so that you can learn from how you respond, and watch your progress. This is essential whether you're working on your own or alongside a therapist. If you see a therapist, you can use this to help keep them updated on how you got on with the exposure that you negotiated in the previous session. You should also monitor whether you responded with any compulsions or safety-seeking behaviours. To help you do this, we have provided a suitable form here, entitled 'Exposure record sheet'; a completed example is shown below, and a further empty form is included at the back of this book.

EXAMPLE EXPOSURE RECORD

Exposure task carried out	Level of discomfort	Duration of discomfort	How did you cope?	Testing your expectations	Next steps
Please write out the date and describe what you actually did.	What was your level of anxiety or discomfort on a scale of 0–10 at the start and when it was at its maximum?	How long did the maximum level of discomfort last for?	What helpful things did you do to tolerate your anxiety? Did you use any unhelpful ways of coping (e.g. any checking, reassurance)?	What did you learn about how your problem works? Did your experience strengthen Theory B?	How might you progress from here, e.g. by repeating, extending or developing this exercise, or moving on to an alternative task?
e.g. I watched and re-watched key scenes in a documentary about dementia	Start: 5 Maximum: 8	10 mins	I tried to think of it like pushing through pain at the gym	Even with something genuinely really sad, I can get stronger in coping with it	I need to repeat this and maybe go and visit a hospital

7. Response Prevention

Response Prevention means not carrying out behaviours such as checking on the internet or seeking (or giving yourself) reassurance. It means learning to tolerate discomfort and uncertainty in a way that helps you overcome your fears. We know it sounds dangerously like telling you to 'just stop it', so we are going to discuss the various approaches. (You might like to search for Bob Newhart's 'Stop It' comedy sketch on the internet.) We'll explain a bit more below.

a) Understand your motivation

Try to understand the motivation to carry out your compulsion or safety-seeking behaviour and use this to help guide you toward facing your fears. For example, is your action motivated to avoid your feared illness? If so, the aim is to try and live with a bit more risk. Is it to do with avoiding the feeling of anxiety? If so, the aim is to tolerate the distress and test out your expectations as to what will happen with those feelings of discomfort. Is it to do with trying to avoid being in a state of doubt or uncertainty? Then your aim, in the service of your mental health, should be to try and take the opportunity to increase your tolerance of doubt.

b) Record the frequency of bodily checking, reassurance, internet searching and self-monitoring

Recording the frequency of a behaviour that is part of maintaining your health anxiety can be really helpful in helping bring about change. Many people find using a tally counter is the most efficient way to do this but you can also use the frequency chart on page 214. Frequency recording has the following advantages:

- The more aware you are, the more you can work to stop it.
- Seeing the frequency reduce can be rewarding feedback and a useful way of recording your progress.
- Now that you are monitoring the frequency of behaviours like checking, reassurance and self-monitoring you are likely to feel more determined to resist them.

c) Reduce the frequency of or time spent on your compulsions

Some people are advised to reduce the frequency of their compulsions gradually (e.g. from checking the degree of tremor from fifty times a day to forty a day) or the amount of time they spend on a compulsion (e.g. 2 hours to 1.5 hours). This is *not* generally recommended as it is incredibly slow and not very effective as you are not learning to tolerate the anxiety from the exposure and test out your predictions. Indeed, you may just speed up your compulsions.

d) Delay the compulsion

This means waiting for say 10 minutes before you do the compulsion. This might then be increased to 20 minutes and so on. This is better than reducing the frequency as it is helping you to tolerate anxiety. It might sometimes be used as a means towards an end. However, it is *not* generally recommended as it does not really help you to test out your prediction in Theory B and is inefficient.

EXERCISE 8.2: FREQUENCY OF CHECKING OR REASSURANCE

Date _____

	Mon	Tues	Wed	Thurs	Fri	Sat	Sun

e) Increase avoidance

If you manage to resist your compulsions, do not compensate by increasing your avoidance. For example, you check your body for cancer less, but you are now avoiding any reminders of cancer in the media. This is not recommended as it just creates another problem. You have to do both – resist compulsions and do exposure, in this case, to the uncertainty of not knowing.

f) Increase exposure after a compulsion

If you can't resist carrying out a compulsion, then the best approach is to 'undo' or spoil it by exposure. For example, if you neutralised an intrusive thought or image about dying, then make sure you bring it back and wish it to happen.

g) Develop an alternative behaviour to seeking or giving yourself reassurance

Seeking or giving reassurance is a type of checking compulsion. For a loved one, just stopping giving reassurance can be fraught with problems. Here are some common problems:

1. Your loved ones know it is unhelpful to give reassurance but feel stuck and unable to cope. A person with health anxiety may become distressed, frustrated, angry and resentful when you just stop giving reassurance.
2. If you just stop giving reassurance, then the health anxiety questioning becomes more subtle or sneakier and a loved one is still drawn into the cycle.

3. It's often impossible to stick to and so it increases the shame on both the person with health anxiety and the loved one.

4. Even if the loved one manages to be consistent in not responding to reassurance-seeking, then the connection between you may become diminished. The person with health anxiety may then seek reassurance from someone else or develop more self-reassurance (which is a mental compulsion) and so the problem has not gone away.

The solution to the person with health anxiety seeking reassurance and to the loved one giving reassurance is to seek and give emotional support. So, the person with health anxiety might seek compassion and care from their loved one when they are wanting reassurance. The loved one needs to respond naturally. The definition of compassion is being sensitive to the person suffering and being deeply committed to relieving that suffering. There are thus two sides to compassion – one is being empathic, sympathetic, caring and soothing. The other is turning towards the distress and not avoiding anxiety. It involves being non-judgemental and acting as if you had courage and wisdom. This may require a bit of planning and role play. It's important that the person with health anxiety and all the family or people who give reassurance have an agreed joint plan of action – the help of a therapist may make it easier.

What this means in practice is the *person with health anxiety* being sensitive to their own suffering and instead of seeking reassurance, labelling the feeling and trying to express what they need (not what they want). They might say something like 'I'm feeling really anxious right now'. If they can, it would help to say what might help: 'Can I have a hug?' or 'Can I have a cup of tea?' 'Can we go for a walk?' Note that there's no request to discuss what they are anxious about – it's like an exposure task, where the person with health anxiety is identifying and labelling their emotion to themselves: 'OK, Anna these are the feelings of anxiety – this is tough, but let's try to just stick with it'. Now if the person with health anxiety can identify what they need (and it is realistic), then the loved one can support them without reassuring them.

Equally, it is important for the person with health anxiety not to become 'rational' and give themselves reassurance. It would be more helpful for them to talk to themselves in a caring and encouraging manner like their relative and not discuss the content of their worry.

Ruminations and rabbit holes

Ruminations or mental compulsions are more difficult to resist than overt compulsions. For ruminations, you need to be clear about:

- exactly what intrusive thoughts or images provoke anxiety
- making sure that these are not linked to trauma memories (e.g. flashbacks) as these require a different approach with a therapist

- how you respond to the thoughts (for example mental reviews of the evidence, self-reassurance, neutralising).

Some ruminations may be trickier and we will try to focus on the ruminations which are characterised by doubt. They are trickier because they are like going down a rabbit hole. In Lewis Carroll's *Alice's Adventures in Wonderland*, the hero of the story, Alice, falls down a rabbit hole and is transported into a surreal land where nothing makes sense. It can be helpful to think of ruminations as rabbit holes into which a person with health anxiety can fall. These rabbit holes are similarly surreal; trying to navigate questions that have no answer can be distressing, trapping a person with health anxiety in a maze. Exploring rabbit holes to find the cause of it all can be unhelpful, sometimes dangerous.

Even if you've managed to successfully navigate your rabbit hole in the past and escaped (maybe having found a satisfactory answer to a doubt or question), was it really helpful to do so in the long term? Or was it more like scratching an itch? If, by diving into the rabbit hole, you'd found a lasting solution to your health anxiety, it's unlikely you would be reading this book.

Try instead to train yourself *to be aware* of your rabbit hole's existence but resist the temptation to fall into it. This involves focusing your attention on the world around you – not the darkness of the rabbit hole that is your mind. Being in your mind is helpful when you have an *actual* problem to solve and can be creative, e.g. how am I going to be a good parent to my children? How can I develop a loving relationship or connect with my partner? So, if you are more aware of the rabbit hole in your landscape, you can either choose to go into the rabbit hole to ruminate in the darkness for hours on end – or you can choose to be in the real world and do the things in life that are important to you despite not knowing an answer to your doubt. It's OK if you choose to go down the rabbit hole, but notice what effect it has on your mood and how it interferes with your life.

It's more helpful to just acknowledge your intrusive thoughts in a detached way – as we've suggested earlier in the book, it can be good to think about your thoughts as being like walking along the side of the road and being aware of the passing traffic, but not trying to stop or control the traffic. You can never get rid of the traffic – remember, your thoughts are normal and we all have doubts. Try to refocus your attention externally on the environment and other practical tasks (such as really listening to someone and responding to them).

Tolerating anxiety

People often ask for techniques to help them cope with or manage their anxiety. However, the process of tolerating means allowing yourself to experience the thoughts and feelings (even when you dislike them or disagree with them) without trying to control or interfere with them. We are sorry, there is no magic wand we can wave; it requires courage. This means feeling the fear yet choosing to act and

DO NOTHING to reduce anxiety or prevent harm from occurring.

A few people struggle to tolerate feeling anxious and try to escape or control their feelings (e.g. with alcohol, substances, food, harming themselves, keeping constantly busy and so on). This may relate to your temperament, having fears of being abandoned and difficulties in relationships with others. Here are some possible solutions that might be helpful for you if you are struggling with tolerating anxiety:

a) Diving reflex

This may be a helpful way of stimulating your vagus nerve, which helps to put a brake on your nervous system: you put your face above your nose to your scalp line in a bucket of very cold water, and this stimulates the diving reflex (like going underwater in a cold pool). You can also achieve the cooling effects by placing an ice pack against your face and briefly holding your breath. The diving reflex slows your heart rate and relaxes your body. This can be helpful when you are very anxious and have the urge to do something unhelpful (e.g. use substances or harm yourself). We don't know how effective it is when you have an urge to do a compulsion, but it may be worth trying.

b) Connection to others

Reach out for relationships and seek support. Healthy connections to others, whether this occurs in person with a hug, over the phone or via texts or social media, can help you tolerate difficult emotions. Relationships can evoke a spirit of playfulness and creativity or can relax us into a trusting bond with another. Remember you can also connect with yourself by rubbing your hands together and over your arms and shoulders and massaging your face.

c) Soothing rhythm breathing

The breath is one of the fastest ways to influence your level of anxiety. The aim is to move your tummy with your breath and to slow your breathing. This will take some time to practise for it to have a benefit when you do exposure tasks. Slow breathing will stimulate the parasympathetic (vagus) nerve, which is like putting a brake on your threat system (the sympathetic nerves). (1) aim to slow your breath to five breaths per minute, (2) spend longer on the out breath. For example, count your in breath to five, hold briefly, and try to exhale to a count of eight to ten. Breathe like you are trying to fog a mirror to create the feeling in the throat but breathe through your nose. Use your lower abdomen breathing rather than upper chest breathing. Using soothing rhythm is unlikely to help unless you practise it a lot beforehand. It is best practised when you have recovered. Practising over time will enable you to breathe in a way that will help you tolerate stress and put a brake on your system in future.

Some examples of putting the principles together

Here are some examples of the characters we introduced in the first chapter using some exposure, alongside some other strategies, to overcome their health anxiety. Once again, it's important to focus not on the particular problem, but on the 'spirit' of breaking free from health anxiety and finding ways of facing your fears.

Adrian's recovery

Adrian was initially very resistant to the notion that he had health anxiety, believing he was being fobbed off by his doctor whom he felt 'doesn't know what else to do with me'. Developing two alternative theories about the nature of his problem was then a crucial first step: Theory A ran 'I've got a heart problem that no one can pin-point', and Theory B ran 'I'm overly preoccupied and anxious and worry that I've got a heart problem'. He then began to consider the possibility that his very consciousness about his heart could be making him more prone to misinterpret normal changes in rhythm as signs of a problem. He demonstrated to himself that if he really concentrated on different body parts, such as his fingertips, he would notice sensations he would otherwise be unaware of.

Adrian then decided to try out treating his problem 'as if' it was an anxiety problem. He educated himself on common symptoms of anxiety, noticing that many of them involved body sensations that he tended to worry about. He began taking regular exercise as part of his deliberate exposure and worked hard to resist his urges to check his pulse and blood pressure or to seek out more information on the internet. Adrian then reduced his self-focus and learned to distance himself from thoughts of having heart disease and not engage with them. He gave his exposure a 'boost' by drinking strong coffee before exercise. As he improved, he took stock of his life, re-focusing himself on what was important to him. He made a will and his preoccupation with his heart slowly decreased. He also took up a new hobby, began to eat more healthily, and lost some weight as part of sensible precautions to look after his heart.

Anne's recovery

Anne recorded the frequency of her checking on a tally counter and began to cut it down. Because her breasts were sore and bruised from her vigorous checking, she readily decided that stopping this should be an early target. She also used a 'responsibility pie chart' on keeping her family happy, to help herself see that the responsibility did not fall wholly on her shoulders and that it would not be the absolute end of the world if she did become ill.

Anne used a cost-benefit analysis chart and reduced her checking. As part of her deliberate exposure she focused on the image of her dying and in her mind made it into a tragic comedy – that she was to die a slow lingering death from breast cancer and before she died both her children and husband would die in a car accident on their way to visit her. She reproduced the original image in a painting of herself dying. She also watched two films which focused on women dying of breast cancer and re-watched the scenes she found most distressing for about half an hour a day for a week. Anne decided to focus upon feeling gratitude for her happy life, and allowed any thoughts about it being spoiled to pass through her mind without engaging with them.

Ibrahim's recovery

At the beginning of his recovery, Ibrahim experimented with *increasing* his attempts to try and control his thoughts to clarify the effect of this strategy on his feelings that his surroundings were unreal. He soon discovered that the more he fought against these experiences the worse he found them. This helped him to become more accepting of his thoughts and feelings. Ibrahim liked the idea of tackling his fears head on and arranged to visit a local psychiatric unit, which upon arrival he found extremely scary. He talked to patients who were recovering from schizophrenia. To his surprise, after about an hour he noticed he felt very much calmer.

To make his exposure more practical, he found as many films as he could that involved mental illness and watched the scenes he found most upsetting again and again until he felt bored with them. He visited the Museum of the Mind at the Bethlem Royal, one of the oldest psychiatric hospitals in the world. He then wrote out a story describing his worst fears happening and read this each day over a two-week period. He found this made it far easier for him to see his thoughts and images as mental events or 'just rubbish that pops into my head because I'm afraid of it'. He wrote and talked about some of his childhood experiences and was able to link some of the fears of losing control with his father.

Victoria's recovery

Victoria's first step was to keep a frequency count of her reassurance-seeking using a tally counter. This helped her to see more clearly just how often she was seeking reassurance and how this might be fuelling her preoccupation. She reduced and eventually stopped researching on the internet and did the same with reassurance-seeking from her parents. Victoria also devoted a relatively small amount of time to attention-training, but she reported that learning to distance herself from her thoughts about disease was the technique she found the most useful.

As part of her exposure, Victoria visited an HIV clinic in a local hospital. She was very struck that although some of the people attending probably did have a blood-borne illness, none of them looked as worried as she did. This helped her to draw a clearer distinction between fear and illness – seeing that, even if you are ill, hours of worry each day is not inevitable. Earlier in her recovery she would say to herself that she was allowed to engage with thoughts about her health only once a week (which she soon discovered she was actually not that interested in doing), and then increased this to once a fortnight, then once a month. She began to re-engage with sports and fitness activities and returned to full-time work. She began to tolerate uncertainty and accepted that if she did have a serious illness she would communicate to her relatives and doctors how she would like to be treated.

Your own plan for overcoming health anxiety

- Having read the examples above, are there any additional exposure tasks you can think of to add to your own list?
- As you deliberately go against avoidance and choose to seek out triggers for your fears, are there any strategies (like checking, self-reassurance or seeking reassurance) that you will need to resist?
- When and where and for how long will you carry out your exposure?
- Where are you going to start?
- Is there anyone you will tell that you are going to start deliberate exposure for your health anxiety, so that they can check-in with you on how you're getting on?

_____

_____

_____

_____

_____

Key points:

- Because health anxiety can involve both your habit mechanisms and your emotional system most people can't just 'stop it'; you're likely to need to put in some deliberate practice to help rehabilitate your mind in order to break free. This will be like doing physiotherapy or training to help you become stronger and/ or more flexible in your mind, in ways that help you overcome your health anxiety.

- This practice is usually called exposure and response prevention (ERP: also see page 194), behavioural experiments or 'exposure' for short.
- This might be by approaching a trigger in real life.
- It might be using words, stories, sounds, images or video from the internet.
- It might be a written story of your own worst fears.
- Exposure can also be repeatedly replaying an audio-recording of you describing your fears out loud.

No matter the form your health anxiety takes, there's almost always some way to deliberately face your fears.

9

Overcoming excessive fear of death

Some people with health anxiety ultimately fear suffering or not being in control of their body (for example through having multiple sclerosis). When this is the case, it may help to volunteer in a hospice for neurological conditions as well as doing some of the other exercises in the previous chapter.

Others are focused on fears about death and dying. If this is true for you, then this chapter may help. It may help you to see how common thoughts and fears of death are experienced so that you learn you are not alone; it should give you some ideas on overcoming an excessive fear of death; and for some readers simply reading and re-reading this chapter will be an excellent way of confronting something that they may normally try to avoid thinking about.

Fears of death are common in the general population and occur much more frequently in people with health anxiety. But fear of death can also occur in people without health anxiety. It is generally more common in women than men. Having strong religious beliefs does not seem to protect people from fears of death. The first step to understanding this fear is to determine the meaning behind it that drives your desire to avoid thinking about your own death.

Depression and suicide

This chapter is not suitable for you at this stage if you are suffering from depression *and* are feeling suicidal. If you have any desire or intention to end your life, even if you have not made plans to do so, we strongly recommend that you seek help from your family doctor or emergency department immediately. A family doctor will be able to offer you diagnosis and further treatment for your depression.

Common beliefs about death

There are very many different types of beliefs that keep fear of death going, and here we will discuss some of the most common ones. Many are linked to an intolerance of uncertainty or 'not knowing' what might happen when you die or after you die.

The process of dying is likely to be very painful and involve a lot of suffering.

> The experience of people who die from terminal illnesses is that they are well supported, and that pain is reasonably well controlled. The issue for some people with a fear of death is the actual moment of dying. There have been reports of people who have

died from a heart attack, for example, and then have been resuscitated, and who have later described death as an extremely pleasant process. This is probably because at the time of death the brain releases its own opiate drug (called endorphins) to give you a warm pleasant feeling, and so this is not something to fear. There are videos on the internet from people who have been resuscitated that may be helpful to watch.

The afterlife may be an experience worse than living.

You might believe that after death you will be a floating soul with thoughts and feelings, unable to control events around you, or that you will be burning in hell. If you believe these thoughts and images to be an accurate prediction of the future (see a description of 'magical thinking' in Chapter 6), then you are *fusing* them with reality and treating them as important as the here and now. Your thoughts and images are just mental events and have no power to predict the future – they just represent your fears. If you believe them, it's very understandable that you will do everything you can to prevent yourself from dying. This in turn can become a preoccupation. You could be extremely self-focused and endlessly analysing and trying to know for certain what will happen when you die. This preoccupation and living in your head will mean that you won't have a life now. However, it is equally likely that when you are dead you will have no thoughts or feelings, so you won't know about it.

After I die, my partner might marry someone I hate or my children won't cope without me as a parent.

This fear might take the form of an intrusive image. Death represents the ultimate in giving up control. Thus, you may try to do everything you can to try to be in control of events after you die (and ruin your life now as everyone gets fed up with your attempts to control everything). It's true that your partner might get a new life if you die and even your children will cope without you as others will rally around to support them. Equally, when you are dead your relatives and friends could dance on your grave if they wanted to and there's nothing you can do about it now. Your worries about what will happen if you die probably tell you more about your relationship with your partner or children now rather than what will happen after your death.

If you are experiencing thoughts or images about what will happen after you die, then just try to experience them without engaging with them and without trying to control them. Do not try to run them on with a happy ending since this just maintains the fear. Detach from such thoughts and keep living life to the full and solve the problems in your relationship with your partner or children.

I have doubts about what will happen after death.

People without strong religious beliefs may have the most difficulty with existential doubts about death. If you are religious, you are likely to have faith in your teachings, although these do not necessarily protect you from fear – we have had many patients with doubts about the teachings of their faith. The problem here is the endless analysis and rumination involved in trying to find an answer. Each answer usually leads to more questions and doubts, leading to a vicious circle. There is of course no answer – if there were, someone would have worked it out before you. The best way of thinking about what it's like to be dead is to think about what it was like before you were born. Enough said?

I might go to hell.

This fear is a little like the existential doubt above about what will happen after death. You may benefit from talking to a minister of your religion about this issue. Hell is not so prominent these days in most religions, and you will probably be told that where you go after your death is not in your control. If you go to hell, then you are very likely to find us there as well, so we can counsel you at the same time. Again, the key issue is to live life to the full now or you will create your hell on Earth now.

I should die at a reasonable old age, and it would be terrible and unfair to die any younger than this.

People with health anxiety know that they must die, but the issue is usually dying 'prematurely'. Unfortunately, there is no law in the universe that says that you must die at a ripe old age. The average age of death may be about seventy-five for men and about seventy-nine for women, but this is an average: some people die much younger, and some people die older. The age of death is of course skewed so that people die from a vast range of ages from childbirth up to seventy-five and equally a number are then bunched up to die between seventy-five and about one hundred. An average means that you are just as likely to die under the age of seventy-five. Even if you follow a healthy lifestyle and there is longevity in your relatives you can be killed in an accident or develop some rare cancer through no fault of your own. Barring accidents, our genes probably largely decide our life expectancy. We ourselves have only a modest influence over when we die. We would of course encourage you to follow a healthy lifestyle of not smoking or using substances, exercising, eating diversely in your food and drinking modestly (so long as the pursuit of a healthy lifestyle does not become excessive and means you don't have a life). However, recognise that there are no rules about whether you should die at an old age. You may or you may not die young – you have a limited influence over the time and date of your death. Overcoming this fear is, again, about giving up control over something that you have a limited influence over.

Consequences of a fear of death

If you fear death or dying, then there are usually two main consequences. The first is that you are likely to avoid triggers that remind you of the idea of your own death. The second is that you may be trying too hard to prevent yourself from dying. These include safety-seeking behaviours that are common in health anxiety. The next sections deal specifically with avoidance of images and ideas about your death. Whereas most phobias are very unlikely to happen, we can say for certain that death will happen – it's just that we don't know when. The solution is to be able to experience and tolerate the distress in the thoughts or images about your death. The secret of life is to live in the moment without making any judgement. The trick is not to focus on what you could have experienced in the past, trying to find reasons for past experiences or what you might experience in the future. Invariably if you fear and worry about death, it leads you to avoid life. These processes will ruin your experience of the present and interfere with your ability to live life to the full.

Exposure exercises

This section should be read after you have read the previous chapter about the principles of exposure and behavioural experiments to test out your predictions. You will recall that worry often leads to inactivity and avoidance of actions that you take to prepare yourself for what is likely. Death is about the only guarantee in life and there are many exercises you can do to prepare for the 'Grim Reaper'. Note that some family members or friends may have their own issues relating to death so don't be surprised if they are unenthusiastic about your doing any of these exercises or think that we (the authors) are just sick. But these exercises really can help with fears of death!

1. Seek inspirational role models who have accepted death gracefully or have used the news that they are going to die to motivate themselves to get the most from their lives in their final months. Randy Pausch's 'Last Lecture' (on childhood dreams) for instance, which can easily be found on the internet, is a truly inspirational example of someone who has come to terms with the fact that he is dying from cancer and has only months to live. You can also read books about death, e.g. *When Breath Becomes Air* by Paul Kalanithi, written before he died of lung cancer, or *Gratitude* by Oliver Sacks, again written as the author approached his death from cancer.

If you have completed this task, take a moment to reflect on how it went. How did it feel to read or listen to people who are facing the end? How did it affect your own attitude to life and death? If you have not done this task, what are the obstacles and how can you solve them?

_____

_____

_____

2. Make your will. This will help you to contemplate your own death – and is important to do even if you don't have a fear of death! If you don't make a will and fall under a bus tomorrow, then your government will decide how your estate is to be divided up (which you may not like). The way of dividing up your estate differs from country to country, but if you leave it up to the government you will not be able, for example, to leave any of your money to a charity for research into health anxiety. Make sure you appoint two executors to ensure your wishes are carried out. You may also make other wishes about a guardian for any children or whom you would like them to be looked after by. Make sure that you write your will assuming you will die tomorrow and review it when your circumstances change.

What was your experience of writing your will?

Or if you have not yet written it, what are the obstacles and how will you solve them?

_____

_____

_____

3. Collect memento mori. Memento mori are artistic or symbolic motifs (like a skull) that remind us of death. It is a Latin phrase which literally means 'remember you must die'. They were widely used in the seventeenth and eighteenth centuries. You can search on the internet for art, sculpture or clothing that usually includes a skull or death head.

   Do you have any memento mori already? If not, what type of objects might be useful for you to collect?

_____

_____

_____

4. Write your obituary or eulogy for your own funeral. This is not actually as ridiculous as it sounds. Doctors are encouraged to write their own obituaries for publications like the *British Medical Journal* and to keep it up to date like a curriculum vitae that they write for job applications. An advantage of writing

your own obituary is that you can make sure your record is accurate. It is then an enormous help to your executor or relative who will have to tell your mourners about your life and what it stood for. It doesn't of course mean that the person who gives your eulogy or writes an obituary doesn't put a different slant on your life. For your purpose of overcoming your fear of death, when you write the obituary make sure that it reads as if you died tomorrow. Write in detail about your life and what you strove for. Tell your executor where you have filed the details about your life and discuss it with a close relative or friend.

What was your experience of writing your obituary or eulogy for your funeral? If you have not done this task, what are the obstacles and how can you solve them?

_____

_____

_____

5. Write out and discuss your wishes for your funeral arrangements. Do you want an ecological funeral? There are many ways of disposing of bodies that are better for the environment than burial. Do you have any wishes about being buried or cremated? If cremated, what would you like done with your ashes?

Again, discussing your wishes and writing them down is important. Even if you don't have a fear of death, if you fail to discuss your wishes then your relatives may do something you would not be happy with. For example, they might arrange a semi-religious funeral in an expensive coffin when you are an atheist and want a biodegradable coffin – or vice versa!

You might want to discuss some of the music that you'd like to have played or the literature to be read. One of us has every intention of asking our children to annoy a few of our relatives with a live jazz band and some John Coltrane – such a shame that we won't be alive to appreciate it! We have also requested for our ashes to be donated to our clinic so they can be kept in the cupboard and taken out for exposure tasks for people with a fear of death and health anxiety. No doubt Health and Safety might have something to say about this, but so much better to overcome your fears of death with the ashes of the authors of the chapter you are reading! It gives a whole new meaning to interactive media. So, if you want to donate your ashes to helping other people suffering from health anxiety or sprinkle them in the River Ganges or shoot them to the stars, write down your preferences and wishes about your final party (and make sure you leave money to pay for it!). This exercise will again help you to think about your own mortality, but it is also a very normal activity.

What was your experience of discussing and writing out your funeral arrangements? If you have not done this task, what are the obstacles and how can you solve them?

_____

_____

_____

6. Throw an anti-necrophobia (or anti-fear of death) party. Again, this is not as ridiculous as it sounds. When one of us had his fiftieth birthday, he threw a party that celebrated death with the most fun possible. There was a Grim Reaper and someone else dressed as the Devil to welcome guests. We had an actor who played a funeral director who kindly measured people up for a coffin and discussed their wishes. There was even a coffin in the garden to try out. One of the band's numbers was to improvise on the Funeral March. After dinner, chocolates consisted of 'obols' (a type of coin) to be put under one's tongue to pay the ferryman, Charon, to take guests across the mythical River Styx to Hades in the garden. All the guests reported having a good time, although we fear some of the people who did not attend may have been very superstitious. We are sure you can think of many equally fun exercises to overcome a fear of death whilst having a good party!

7. Expose yourself to specific triggers that remind you of death. There may be many different triggers. You might avoid:

    - taking a route that passes a cemetery
    - funerals
    - reading obituaries or about deaths in the media
    - watching movies or TV programmes that involve death or dying
    - reading books about people who are dying or have died
    - discussing death
    - having a pet (which some people avoid as pets often die before their owners).

All these need to be added to your hierarchy (see Chapter 8) for exposure and done repeatedly until you can tolerate your distress and have tested out your expectations. You can add to your hierarchy a personification of death like the 'Grim Reaper' or put up pictures of hell in your bedroom; visit a grave or memorial stone of someone in the family; visit a funeral parlour; read the accounts and blogs of people suffering from terminal illnesses and who eventually die. Death is not something most of us want to happen, but the issue is learning to tolerate the anxiety and testing out your expectations.

What activities did you do for exposure? If you

have not done this task, what are the obstacles and how can you solve them?

_____

_____

_____

8. Write a story about your own death. Write it in the first person and in the present tense as if it is happening now from a field perspective (that is, through your own eyes rather than observing yourself). Write a step-by-step account using as many different senses as possible (what you see, what you can touch, what you hear, what you smell). Be sure to focus on your specific fears (suffocating, for instance) and that it finishes at your death (and not an afterlife).

9. Have you had any experiences of death connected with a close relative or friend that have been traumatic or bad? This would make your fears very understandable and likely to be still influencing the present. If there are aspects of their death you are avoiding, then you may benefit from seeing a therapist to talk through these issues or use imagery to re-experience them, to lose the sense of nowness about the image and understand some of the meaning that is linked to your relative or friend's death. This may be contributing to some of the beliefs and feelings that you currently experience and may be keeping your fear going.

10

Keeping health anxiety at bay

Make a written summary of the gains you have made and how you made them. In the future you may need to recall what you did, so write down a summary of how you have been overcoming your health anxiety using the exercise below. As well as being extremely useful, this exercise can also help you feel justifiably proud of the changes you've made.

Key techniques checklist

- Have you removed all the safety behaviours (behavioural and mental) and avoidance behaviours that were driven by your health anxiety? If not, what can you do to continue to reduce them (e.g. resisting the urges to check or seek reassurance and exposure for avoidance)?
- Have you managed to reduce your attentional focus on your body and re-trained your attention to focus more readily on the outside world and the here and now?

- Have you focused your mind upon your valued directions in life and begun to live more consistently with these values?
- Have you learned to normalise bodily and mental sensations and reduced your tendency to jump to conclusions about them?
- Can you 'detach' from anxiety-provoking thoughts and allow them to pass through your mind without engaging with them?
- Have you managed to reduce your fears of thoughts, doubts, images and sensations? If not, what can you do to reduce these further (e.g. exposure and behavioural experiments)?
- Have you 'filled the gap' left by your health anxiety with interesting, pleasurable, absorbing or satisfying activities (e.g. new hobbies, work, building relationships, following your valued directions)?

What have been the most helpful things you've learned that have helped you overcome your health anxiety?

_____

_____

_____

What have been the most helpful techniques you've applied for benefit in the long term for overcoming your health anxiety?

_____

_____

_____

One of the biggest mistakes we see people make is the decision to settle for 'manageable health anxiety'. In our view this is a bit like trying to aim to stay 'a bit pregnant' – sooner or later, things are going to develop further! Such a decision leaves you vulnerable to relapse. So, in the same way that a bad back sufferer needs to strengthen his back and tummy muscles, people who are recovering from health anxiety need to strengthen their psychological capabilities such as tolerating doubt, non-excessive responsibility, de-catastrophising, risk-taking and flexible thinking. They must remain aware of their vulnerability.

Some people may ultimately need to accept a long-term, reduced, 'manageable' level of health anxiety, but this will only happen if they continue to work at minimising it and keeping psychologically healthy. Inevitably you will have setbacks from time to time. Note there is an important distinction to be made between a relapse and a setback. A relapse means a 'back to the beginning' slip in your health anxiety, whereas a setback is a slip backward on the road to recovery. The good news is that neither is a hopeless situation, but by dealing effectively with setbacks you can dramatically reduce the chances of a relapse.

Setbacks are a normal part of recovery

The 'two steps forward, one step back' experience is common in many endeavours, and overcoming health anxiety is no different. Don't panic if you slip back but do try to see if you can learn anything about why you slipped backwards. A few examples are:

- Encountering a previously avoided trigger, which can now become part of your exposure hierarchy;
- Allowing yourself 'small amounts of ritual', such as a 'quick check', which then escalates, serving as a reminder of how firmly you need to resist rituals;
- Discovering that you've been relying on certain conditions to do exposure and response prevention (e.g. after discussing it with someone) and then finding it difficult to manage without these conditions (in this case you need to redesign your exposures to be more independent);
- Having become complacent about exposure and response prevention without having done sufficient work to remove the fear, allowing your fear to grow.

Whilst setbacks are disappointing, you can make the most of them if you use them as an opportunity to learn about the strengths and weaknesses of your recovery and then make a plan that builds on your strengths as well as minimising your weaknesses. Try to make a plan on how to deal with setbacks by considering the following.

1. What events or situations might trigger a setback?

How could you plan to tackle these events or situations to minimise their impact? What could you do to practise coping with them?

_____

_____

_____

_____

_____

_____

2. Act sooner rather than later

To reduce the chances of a setback becoming more serious it's helpful to take action to tackle it as early as you can. What might be early warning signs that your health anxiety is beginning to creep back in?

_____

_____

_____

_____

_____

_____

3. *In order for you to maintain your gains what are the main things you need to work at?*

_____

_____

_____

_____

_____

_____

11

Supporting someone overcoming health anxiety

This chapter is primarily written for family members or friends of people with health anxiety. It will be of most help if the person who suffers from health anxiety has read through this book and is actively seeking to overcome his or her problem. If this is the case, the most helpful thing you, as a helper, can do is become an ally for the individual in overcoming their health anxiety, if he or she wishes you to.

To recover from health anxiety, lots of the right kind of hard work and brain-training is needed. However, the fact remains that it's not how much you (the therapist, partner, relative, friend, doctor, helper, etc.) want the person with health anxiety to change that counts, but rather that the person with health anxiety has to be in the driving seat. Even where professional therapy is concerned, you can only take a horse to water – you cannot make it drink. The key is to encourage the person with health anxiety to 'try out' treating their problem 'as if' it's a problem of worrying about their health to see how it works out. You can say that you are prepared to support them if they are prepared to fully commit themselves and do the exercises consistently for at least three months. If the approach doesn't work, then they can always go back to seeing more doctors and having further tests.

In cognitive behavioural therapy (CBT), the person who acts as an ally in this way is sometimes called a 'co-therapist'. Such allies can be of enormous value and can help in numerous ways. If you decide to be an ally or co-therapist for a person with health anxiety, it will make sense for both of you to work through this book and review it together as you progress. However, be aware that you, the co-therapist, may come to feel that the person you are trying to help is over-involved with monitoring their homework or progress. If this happens, both of you will need to re-negotiate your degree of involvement.

General guidelines for relatives

Know your enemy!

If you are a relative or a friend of someone with health anxiety, and especially if you are the partner of someone with health anxiety, get to know as much as you can about the condition (e.g. by reading books like this one), the common behaviours and the treatments available. It's worth emphasising three key points:

- However odd the behaviours may seem, they are just part of health anxiety. Health anxiety is not a sign of madness – it's simply a disorder, of the kind that can affect many people at some stage in their lives. The behaviour of someone with health anxiety is neither 'bad' nor done to annoy you.

• If you have a relative or partner with health anxiety, it's still important to set consistent boundaries with behaviours that are unrelated to health anxiety, and to problem-solve health anxiety behaviour where it impinges on your family life (for example, the length of time the person spends researching information on the internet).

• Health anxiety is not something that can be easily stopped. It will take time, commitment and the right guidance to improve everyone's quality of life. Each person needs to overcome his or her problems at their individual pace, even though this may be a lengthy process. Avoid comparing your relative or friend to other individuals with a mental health problem or indeed without it.

Avoid the blame game

No one should be blamed for health anxiety – it's not the fault of the person who has it, and nor is it the fault of a relative. If you are a parent there is no need to feel guilty for 'causing' health anxiety, even if there is a possible genetic link. If you start blaming your genes, then you can go all the way back to Adam and Eve!

Encourage your relative to seek help

Encourage your relative with health anxiety to try out the principles explained in this book, and to seek professional help with therapy or medication if they need it. Support them in either or both routes and do everything you can to help them change. This means:

- helping them to understand and define their problems clearly
- if they want you to, being an ally as described above
- encouraging them to persist with their treatment and praising any improvement, however small.

Don't participate in health anxiety

Families should not try to adapt their ways of doing things to accommodate a relative's worries. Don't put family life on hold. Accept that health anxiety may complicate family life, but get on with it anyway, and encourage your relative to maintain as normal a lifestyle as possible:

- Don't collaborate in trying to find 'magic solutions', such as cutting details about health scans out of the paper or offering to pay for private doctors' appointments or provide a loan.
- Don't provide reassurance. This is of course easier said than done, but we discuss alternatives below.
- Don't take on the responsibilities of the person with health anxiety (unless of course you are a parent of a child).

- Don't make excuses for them (for their being late for work or for an appointment, for example).
- If necessary, compromise in the short term in the way we have described but draw the line when new avoidance behaviours and safety behaviours start.

If you have been participating in your relative's health anxiety up to now, start to find ways of changing this:

- If the person is in therapy, ask your relative if you can see the therapist with him or her and discuss a programme of reducing your involvement in your relative's health anxiety.
- If the person is not in therapy, try to negotiate a programme of gradual withdrawal from the person's reassurance-seeking and checking safety and avoidance behaviour before you implement it.
- Make sure that you communicate that you are changing your involvement to help rather than punish.
- Practise providing emotional support and encouragement rather than reassurance. 'I understand Paul, this is tough but try to stick with your anxiety and it will get easier.' Ask your relative for the alternative explanation (Theory B) and encourage them to act as if it is true even if they don't yet believe it.
- Help your relative to see the downside of you accommodating your avoidance and safety behaviours and the effect on your relationship. Highlight how long the effect of the reassurance lasts for and what the

effect is on their doubts. In other words, try not to respond to the content of their worries but focus them more on questioning the process of what they are doing (e.g. use questions that help your relative reflect on the effect of giving reassurance on your relationship and on their health anxiety).

Anticipate how you will deal with your relative becoming stressed or irritated by your new way of responding and have a plan that you can both agree upon if he or she becomes aggressive or angry. You may have to be very persistent until requests for reassurance stop happening, because if you respond just once, it immediately becomes more likely that they will involve you again.

Remember:

- Individuals with health anxiety will not come to any harm because of anxiety, though they may be distressed in the short term.
- Accommodating rituals and avoidance means that you are helping to fuel health anxiety in the long term – and you are not taking care of yourself. It may feel as if you're protecting yourself from stress and helping someone with health anxiety, but the effect can be the opposite.
- What is good for the family is good for the person with health anxiety, and this can only occur when no one else engages in the health anxiety. A family that is pulling together can provide better support for your

relative with health anxiety. Its members can also better support each other and solve problems more efficiently.

Be a coach and cheerleader

You and your relative both need to see health anxiety, not the individual experiencing it, as your shared enemy. Approach the problem as a team, working together. As your relative improves, see yourself as a coach shouting encouragement from the sidelines, or cheerleading, as you become less involved. Enthusiasm, understanding and emotional support really are the best help you can provide.

Look after your own needs

You need to follow your own interests and have your own sources of support. At times you may need time out (or respite care). When this happens, tell your relative that you need a break but that you have not given up on them, and try to get others to help in your place.

Feelings such as guilt, sadness and anger are normal in those caring for a relative with any long-term disability.

- Try not to engage in self-pitying thoughts such as 'Why me?' or 'Poor me, I don't deserve to have health anxiety in the family'. These will only make you feel worse and feed another vicious circle.
- Try to detach yourself emotionally from your relative's health anxiety and take it less personally.

- If you're not coping emotionally or it is affecting other areas of your life, seek help. There may be a local caregivers' group or, even better, a group for caregivers of individuals with health anxiety. Alternatively, see your family doctor for a referral or go directly to a therapist.

De-catastrophise anxiety and discomfort

We've met many family members who seem to share the view of people with health anxiety that any anxiety or discomfort should be avoided and have even been critical of CBT because it requires a tolerance of discomfort. In some cases this is entirely understandable, given the profound distress that the individual with health anxiety, whom they care about, experiences as they wrestle with a doubt or intrusive thoughts.

But some families share 'rules' about emotions that can be *unhelpful* in overcoming health anxiety. For example, they believe that:

- Emotions are a sign of weakness and should be controlled.
- If something upsets you, don't think about it.
- Being upset is terrible, and it's important to do something to make yourself feel better as soon as possible.
- If something bothers you, you should do something to take your mind off it.
- You should be careful about showing that you feel upset to other people in case they use it against you.

- If you get too upset it could make you ill, so it's best to avoid intense emotions.

These rules are unhelpful since they interfere with a person's ability to recover from health anxiety. They are sometimes explicitly taught; at other times they are taught by the way a family or person within that family behaves.

If you think you or your family share any rules like these, which might make experiencing emotions even harder, try to communicate to the person with health anxiety the message that you are confident that feeling short-term distress is a sensible and helpful thing when overcoming health anxiety.

Be prepared for setbacks

It's likely that on some days your relative will be better able to deal with symptoms than on others. It will be harder for both of you at certain times – for example, when either of you is feeling tired or stressed by other problems. Setbacks are to be expected and to a certain extent can be planned for. Taking time out can be helpful at these points.

Each person with health anxiety will need to overcome their problems at their own pace, even though this may be a lengthy process. It's entirely normal to experience setbacks along the road to recovery. Don't lose heart. You can help by staying optimistic and encouraging the person to keep trying. You probably won't see the hundred times that health anxiety doesn't get in the way, but you are bound to notice the time that it does!

Keep a sense of humour

People with health anxiety are often aware of the humorous aspects of their worries. However, it is very important that friends and relatives resist any temptation to mock the person with health anxiety for their symptoms because this may cause additional stress, shame and embarrassment.

Keep communicating

Make sure that you keep talking both with your relative who has health anxiety and with everyone else in your family.

- Remember that you may need help and support yourself.
- Make sure that you continue to do things you enjoy and have people to talk to about your own feelings and concerns.
- Eventually, you may decide that, for the sake of your own mental health, you can't carry on caring for your relative with health anxiety. In that case you'll need to communicate as a family and get help from the local services.

What if a relative plays down the problem?

If your relative insists that health anxiety is having hardly any effect on their life, there are various things you can do to encourage them to face up to the problem and seek help. Try to find out:

- what their real feelings are about having such a problem (shame, for example, can make people very reluctant to acknowledge it; see Chapter 1 in this book)
- what they fear
- and/or what doubts they have about therapy or change.

Ensure that as a family, or if possible as a wider group, including friends, you take a consistent approach, and that nobody is accommodating the health anxiety. Agree upon your message, and if necessary talk to the individual both within the family (or wider) group and with a mental health professional.

One person in the group might draw up, along with the relative with health anxiety, a list of costs (or disadvantages) and benefits (advantages) of:

a) staying the way they are, or
b) engaging in a programme of therapy.

A blank copy of the cost-benefit analysis form can be found in Appendix 2 at the end of this book. Each of the costs and benefits may be divided into those for the 'self' and those for 'others'. Even if your relative sees few disadvantages in staying in the same condition, you can emphasise the costs of health anxiety to others in the family and the benefits to themselves in the long term. Continue to emphasise that you will still provide support and help during therapy. If your relative finally agrees to seek help, discuss the time frame within which this can be done, and the process it will involve.

What if a relative refuses to seek help?

If your relative has very severe health anxiety, continues to refuse help and you decide that you cannot go on any longer with things the way they are, you will need to explore your own options, such as finding your relative independent living arrangements by getting help from your local mental health services.

Local mental health services do not always respond positively to requests for help with these cases. The main priority for a psychiatrist in public health services is patients with 'severe mental illness', especially those who may be suicidal or a danger to the community. UK and US mental health law allows a patient to be detained in hospital against their will in certain circumstances; but in the absence of a risk to themselves or self-neglect, patients with health anxiety are unlikely to be admitted to a hospital and would, in any case, be unlikely to benefit much from admission to the average acute psychiatric ward. Short-term in-patient care in a specialist unit where the staff are used to dealing with health anxiety and OCD and where regular CBT is available, is more likely to be helpful. In others a trial of medication may be given against a person's will, which can be helpful to some people, especially those who have lost touch with reality or are severely depressed.

It must be emphasised, though, that CBT is powerless without the cooperation of a person with health anxiety. It is both unethical and counterproductive to forcibly expose someone to feared situations or activities. Therapists may encourage and challenge a patient but would never force exposure or spring something on their patient unannounced. Nor should you ever do this to a relative with health anxiety. A programme of CBT has to be followed voluntarily, and the motivation has to come from the patient, if it is to be ethical and effective.

Remember: Recovery from health anxiety is a process

When your relative or friend is recovering, you may expect everything to go back to how it used to be. Yet this may not be how it happens at all, and the family may need to go through various stages of adjustment. This is normal. Each person will adjust and recover at a different rate. You may want to see health anxiety as something that is 'over' or 'finished' but remember that setbacks are part of the process.

In summary, health anxiety can have a profound effect on the person with health anxiety and on the person or people who look after them. However, though the situation may sometimes be difficult, it is never hopeless and there is a lot that you can do as a team to help each other.

12

A guide to medical treatments for health anxiety

In this chapter, we review some of the main medical and other novel treatments for health anxiety. The two main choices for help in overcoming health anxiety are cognitive behavioural therapy (CBT) and medication. Both have a substantial amount of evidence to recommend them. CBT and medication can be used alone or combined. However, because improvement from medication generally depends on continuing to take the medication, CBT is the preferred initial treatment, especially in mild to moderate health anxiety. Guidelines generally recommend medication as an *additional* treatment if you fail to make progress with CBT, if your health anxiety is more severe or if you are also significantly depressed.

Medication vs CBT

You may find it difficult to obtain CBT because of long waiting lists or other restrictions in public medicine. We think it's important not to give up accessing CBT, but you may be offered medication before you receive it. In the short term, CBT and medication are probably just as effective as each other, and combining the treatments probably does not have a lot of advantage for *most* people with mild to moderate health anxiety. We don't yet know if this is true in the long term (e.g. a year or two later).

Expert opinion is that individuals with severe health anxiety on average make better progress with a combination of CBT and medication. Unfortunately, research does not yet tell us who is more likely to benefit from adding medication to CBT. Whatever treatment you decide to take, make sure you monitor your progress with the rating scales in this book.

Should I take medication?

There exist commonly held misconceptions that can bias a decision on medication which we will tackle now. These are often variations on the following:

1. *'Taking medication would be like cheating and would show I was weak. A recovery would only count if I do it without any assistance from drugs.'* Once again, notice the rather black-or-white thinking contained in this view. Health anxiety is just a condition, no more significant than any other medical condition. That you have it, or how you recover from it, does not define you.

2. *'Taking medication could cause side effects that would be unbearable.'* Later in this chapter we shall cover the

possible side effects and what you can do to minimise them. When deciding about medication, remember to factor in the possible effect of not taking medication and the continuing impairment in your life. Furthermore, if you experience a side effect which cannot be managed then usually (with medical advice) you can stop the medications and it will go away.

3. *'Taking an antidepressant is not necessary since I am not depressed.'* Health anxiety medications are often referred to as 'antidepressants', but they are actually better at reducing anxiety than depression. This makes them effective for people with health anxiety who do *not* have depression.

This section aims to help you make an informed choice about whether you wish to take medication for health anxiety by looking at the potential benefits and disadvantages. We shall also discuss some of the other medications used for health anxiety when first-choice drugs do not work. This chapter was up to date when the book was published. Bear in mind that new information may have come to light since then.

Which type of medication should I take for my health anxiety?

First choice: SSRI Medication

The best evidence for medication for health anxiety is a class of drug called 'Selective Serotonin Reuptake Inhibitors' (or

SSRIs for short) (see Table 12.1 on page 270). When medications are referred to as 'serotonergic' it means that the drugs act on serotonin nerve endings in the brain. 'Selective' refers to the fact that they act on serotonin nerve endings rather than others such as noradrenaline or histamine nerve endings. In Table 12.1, Clomipramine is not strictly an SSRI as it is regarded as a potent serotonergic drug and not as selective. 'Reuptake Inhibitor' refers to the way the drug acts: it helps to stop serotonin being taken back up into the nerve, increasing the concentration of free serotonin available.

This in turn helps to increase the messages passing along certain pathways in the brain and to reduce anxiety. Cast your mind back to Chapter 5 where we described the causes of health anxiety and the threat system designed to keep you safe. This causes an excessive load as another part of your brain is desperately trying to reduce your anxiety. There is no evidence of a defect which the SSRI can be used to correct. SSRIs probably enhance the *normal* activity of the brain. SSRIs are widely used in the treatment of depression and anxiety disorders. A family doctor may prescribe the drug or may refer you to a psychiatrist who will be more aware of the doses required and can give you an opportunity to discuss your issues in more detail.

Controlled trials, in which an SSRI is compared to a placebo (or dummy pill), show that about two-thirds (66 per cent) of health anxiety patients who received an SSRI make improvements compared to about 10 per cent of patients who received a placebo. This means that nearly a third of patients do not experience any significant improvement. *On average*, symptoms reduce by half so that some patients may get no benefit while at the other extreme some may become symptom free. Even if the medication is of benefit, it will not work right away. Most people notice some improvement in their symptoms after about four weeks, while maximum benefit occurs for most people within twelve weeks. *It is therefore important to continue to take your medication at the highest dose you can tolerate for at least twelve weeks before judging how effective it has been.* When making a judgement about effectiveness, always compare the score on a rating scale before and after taking the drug. Ideally take a drug when you are not receiving any CBT, to judge its effectiveness. For some people, progress continues to occur after twelve weeks before reaching a plateau.

All the SSRIs are probably equally effective for health anxiety overall, but any one person may respond better to one SSRI rather than another. The initial choice will depend upon side effects or the personal preference of the prescribing doctor. If you or someone in your family did well or poorly with a medication in the past, this may influence the choice. If you have medical problems (e.g. with sleeping) or are taking another medication, these factors may influence your doctor's choice so that side effects and possible drug interactions are minimised. For example, *citalopram* and *escitalopram* are usually better choices if you are on other drugs that might interact with an SSRI. Escitalopram is similar to citalopram. Citalopram is a mixture of two molecules, which are identical except that they are mirror images of each other. Escitalopram is the molecule that has the serotonin action and is available without a redundant molecule, which has no serotonin action. The result is the same, but escitalopram *may* have slightly fewer side effects.

There are some differences between the other SSRIs. For example, *fluoxetine* takes longer to be metabolised by the body. Thus, if you forget a dose one day, you can get away with it because fluoxetine does not vanish from the blood when you stop taking it. It also tends to be easier to stop. However, it is important to keep in mind that some people with health anxiety may not respond well to SSRIs.

In general, most SSRIs do not interact with small amounts of alcohol, and you may drink safely if you keep your intake to a minimum. However, people's reactions to alcohol do vary when taking an SSRI and some can become more aggressive or sedated. Excessive alcohol can also be a factor in depression and will interfere in any therapy programme. Compared with the older antidepressants, SSRIs are considered safer in overdose because they have few side effects on the heart.

What dose of an SSRI should I be prescribed?

You should discuss the following advice with your doctor. The normal starting dose and suitable target doses of the SSRI medications are listed in Table 12.1. If you can, it's important to try a higher dose because for many people with health anxiety a greater improvement is made with the higher doses. When progress is slow, there is some evidence that increasing the dose above the target dose may give better results.

If you experience significant side effects, you can always start on a lower dose and build up slowly. It used to be possible to prescribe citalopram or escitalopram at a higher dose (for example citalopram 60mg and escitalopram 30mg), but the manufacturer now advises against this in some countries, as it may very rarely affect the heart rhythm. However, this is disputed in scientific circles. It is recommended that those on a higher dose have an ECG to measure their heart rhythm before and after increasing the dose and at regular intervals thereafter.

The target dose for fluoxetine is listed below at 60mg because this is the maximum recommended in the UK. However, in the USA and other countries the maximum licensed dose is 80mg.

Table 12.1: SSRIs and potent SSRIs used for health anxiety

Chemical name	UK trade name	USA trade name	Usual starting dose	Target dose	Liquid preparation
Citalopram	Cipramil	Celexa	20mg	40mg	Yes
Clomipramine	Anafranil	Anafranil	50mg	225mg	No
Escitalopram	Cipralex	Lexapro	10mg	20mg	Yes
Fluoxetine	Prozac	Prozac	20mg	60mg	Yes
Fluvoxamine	Faverin	Luvox	50mg	200mg	No
Paroxetine	Seroxat	Paxil	20mg	40mg	Yes
Sertraline	Lustral	Zoloft	50mg	200mg	Yes

At what time of day should I take an SSRI?

It is usually advised to take an SSRI in the morning after food to reduce the risk of nausea. About 10 to 15 per cent of people on an SSRI feel a bit drowsy and another 5 to 15 per cent cannot sleep. The problem can sometimes be resolved by changing the time of day you take your medication (take it at night, for example, if it makes you drowsy). Fluvoxamine is more likely to cause sleepiness and may be best taken at night.

Will an SSRI have side effects?

Side effects of SSRIs depend on the dose of your medication, how long you have been taking it for and your own genetic makeup. Most people find side effects are minor irritations that usually decrease after a few weeks. They do not usually pose a problem for people who need to take a drug in the long term. The worst side effects usually occur in the first few days or weeks. Because it takes up to twelve weeks for the full benefits of the medication to become clear, it is in that early period when you can't see any improvement and you may be experiencing side effects that you are most likely to stop taking the drug. There is one side effect that does not tend to diminish over time: sexual difficulties. We will discuss below how these might be improved. Side effects that persist including those of a sexual nature will decrease when you stop taking the medication.

You are more likely to experience side effects if you are on a higher dose or if your dose has been rapidly increased.

If you are unable to tolerate the medication, you can try reducing the dose and then increasing it to the previous level more slowly. For example, if you find that you are feeling nauseous after a few days of taking fluoxetine 20mg, you can reduce the dose to 10mg (using the liquid form) for a week or two and then increase it to 20mg again when your body has become more accustomed to the drug. If you are very sensitive to side effects your doctor may start you on a lower dose as a liquid and increase it very slowly. For example, you might start on 2mg of fluoxetine and increase by 2mg per week. Another alternative is to switch to a different SSRI altogether.

Is there anything I can do to reduce side effects of SSRI medication?

We have listed below the most common side effects of SSRIs and how to deal with them. Most will go away after a few weeks, and all will stop if you decide to discontinue the drug slowly under guidance from your doctor.

1. Nausea

Nausea (feeling sick) is the most common but transitory side effect of an SSRI and affects about 25 per cent of patients taking an SSRI compared to about 10 per cent of those on a placebo. Fluvoxamine may be slightly more likely than the other SSRIs to cause it. Nausea can be minimised by taking the drug after food. Alternatively, halve the dose for a couple of weeks and then slowly increase it back to the normal dose. If the nausea still persists then an anti-nausea drug may help, as may switching to an alternative SSRI. Nausea generally improves over time.

2. Diarrhoea or constipation

SSRIs can cause diarrhoea in up to 15 per cent of patients taking an SSRI compared to about 5 per cent taking a placebo. For diarrhoea, always drink plenty of water or take rehydration sachets. Diarrhoea can be minimised by drinking plenty of apple juice (which contains pectin) or the use of a drug such as loperamide or bismuth subsalicylate (Pepto-Bismol). Remember that diarrhoea can also occur as a result of severe anxiety or feelings of disgust.

Constipation occurs in 5 per cent of patients taking an SSRI. Constipation may be improved by having plenty of fruit and fibre in your diet. If altering your diet does not help, then bulking agents such as Fybogel or medicines like lactulose or macrogol may help. For both diarrhoea and constipation, you should drink at least 2 litres of water a day.

3. Headache

Up to 20 per cent of patients taking an SSRI find they develop headaches. Headache is also a common symptom of tension and occurs in about 15 per cent of patients taking a placebo. Symptoms of headache can usually be helped by drinking water and taking simple painkillers such as paracetamol and should decrease after a few weeks of taking an SSRI. Ibuprofen or similar anti-inflammatory drugs are not recommended with SSRIs as they can increase the risk of bleeding. Headaches tend to improve over time.

4. Excessive sweating

Excessive sweating occurs in about 10 per cent of patients taking an SSRI compared to 5 per cent taking a placebo. There is no easy solution to this problem although it should decrease over time. Remember, sweating may also be a feature of anxiety. You could try reducing the dose, but this may worsen your health anxiety. A low dose of an anticholinergic drug such as benztropine may be helpful to combat sweating.

5. Dry mouth

Dry mouth affects about 10 per cent of patients taking an SSRI compared with 5 per cent taking a placebo. Sucking on sugarless gum may stimulate production of saliva or you could try a spray or pastilles that can be bought over the counter to provide artificial saliva. Make sure you drink plenty of water. Again, the symptoms usually decrease over time.

6. Tremor

Shakiness or tremor occurs in about 10 per cent of patients taking an SSRI and 3 per cent on a placebo. A beta-blocker (e.g. propranolol) may reduce tremor if it is severe.

7. Sedation or insomnia

About 10 to 20 per cent of patients on an SSRI feel sedated

and another 5 to 15 per cent cannot sleep. The problem can sometimes be resolved by changing the time of day you take your medication (take it at night, for example, if it makes you drowsy) or taking a different SSRI altogether. Fluvoxamine is more likely to cause sleepiness and may be best taken at night. If you cannot sleep, one solution may be to take a sedative drug to help you sleep in the short term.

8. Emotional numbness

Some patients feel emotionally numb or 'spaced out' on an SSRI. This potential side effect seems to be related to the dose, so a lower dose may improve things (but it may worsen the health anxiety). If you stop taking the drug, your feelings return to normal.

9. Sexual problems

Sexual side effects can take the form of delayed ejaculation in men and an inability to reach an orgasm in women. SSRIs can also occasionally cause both men and women to lose their libido although this is complicated to assess in the presence of depression. Men might find it helpful to check their testosterone level. Adding testosterone gel can sometimes lead to improvement in sexual function in men with low testosterone levels. Women are more complicated!

Sometimes the sexual side effects of SSRIs can be solved with a lower dose of medication. Omitting or delaying a dose (for example not taking it in the morning) before any sexual activity in the evening may be helpful. You can then take the dose after the sexual activity. However, some SSRIs lead to side effects if you omit a dose (e.g. paroxetine). Missing the drug more than once a week risks the return of health anxiety symptoms. Also omitting the drug once a week does not seem to improve libido (only delay in reaching an orgasm).

Another option is to try an alternative SSRI, but it may have the same effect. Sertraline, citalopram or escitalopram have been associated with fewer sexual problems than other SSRIs, so it might be worth switching to one of these if another one is causing problems. There is some evidence for the use of Viagra (sildenafil) or Cialis (tadalafil) for men and women. These drugs are reported as successful in reversing sexual side effects of SSRIs in some men when they are taken regularly. The dose of Viagra is 50mg to be taken one hour before sexual activity. If this does not improve things or gives only a partial response, you could try increasing it to 100mg. Some patients with heart conditions will not be able to take it. The possible side effects of Viagra include headache, flushing and dizziness. Other case reports have included adding another class of antidepressant to the SSRI, such as trazodone (at a low dose of 100mg) or mirtazapine (at a low dose of 7.5–15mg) or buspirone (20–60mg a day) in both men and women, or bupropion (20–60mg a day) in women. Trazodone or mirtazapine are best taken at night as they tend to increase sedation.

There may be other factors linked to sexual problems, some of which may be possible to treat. These include the nature of your relationship, depression, alcohol and smoking.

10. Loss of appetite

Symptoms of loss of appetite and weight loss occur in about 5 to 10 per cent of patients taking SSRIs. Reducing the dose can halt this effect, though it usually improves over time anyway. Some SSRIs can also cause mild weight gain in the long term, and you may need to adjust your diet and exercise programme. Depression and inactivity will also contribute to weight gain.

11. Nervousness or agitation

Some people feel more anxious or 'wired' especially when starting an SSRI. It can be difficult to tell the difference between the anxiety that comes from the health anxiety and what might be caused by the drug. If it is caused by the drug, then it may be solved by (a) switching to a different SSRI or (b) trying a lower dose or (c) adding an additional drug in the short term. The feeling of increased anxiety is usually temporary and will subside over time. *Rarely* the feeling of agitation can develop into an abnormal mood of elation or irritability, your speech becomes pressured, you feel as if you do not need any sleep and you feel you are 'on the go' all the time. This is called a state of mania and you are likely to need to stop taking the SSRI.

Summary

Whenever side effects are a problem, always discuss them with your doctor. The doctor may advise you either (a) to reduce the dose, (b) to try a different SSRI, (c) to add another medication to counteract side effects such as insomnia or sexual problems, or (d) to wait and see, as many of the side effects improve over time.

Stopping an SSRI

When you stop taking an SSRI, you may experience symptoms for a few days or weeks. These can include dizziness, sleep disturbances, agitation or anxiety, nausea, excessive sweating and numbness. These are not the same as the withdrawal symptoms that can occur with minor tranquillisers (drugs of dependence), in which symptoms of rebound anxiety may persist over many months. It is, however, sensible to reduce SSRIs gradually over several weeks when you do cease taking one. This will also help to reduce the risk of relapse. If the symptoms persist when the lower dose range of the drug is reached, then it may be a good idea to halve it before stopping it completely. Fluoxetine lasts longer in the body than other SSRIs before it is metabolised. One way of reducing this drug gently is to take it on alternate days.

Fluoxetine is the least likely SSRI to cause such symptoms and paroxetine the most likely due to the different rates of breakdown in the body. For example, fluoxetine has a longer-lasting effect in the body which means the body has more time to re-adjust, whereas a shorter-acting drug like paroxetine can have a more profound effect because the drug leaves the system quickly. Most symptoms can be minimised by reducing the drugs slowly and this should be done under the guidance of your doctor. If you are on a high dose, the usual advice is to reduce it by about 25 per cent every month.

What if I miss a dose?

If you miss a dose for one day, then it's quite safe to recommence on the previous dose you were taking. You are at risk of symptoms described above if you run out of a prescription and stop from a high dose. If you stop a high dose for two days or more, it may be better to go back to the starting dose and increase over the following week to your current dose. Some drugs such as fluoxetine are easier to miss as they take a long time to metabolise.

How long do I need to take medication for?

Relapse in health anxiety is common when you stop taking medication *and* especially if you have had no CBT. If relapse does occur, it usually does so within two to four months of stopping an SSRI. The risk of relapse will partly depend on the natural pattern of your health anxiety without treatment. For example, if you are lucky enough to have had a single episode of health anxiety, then the condition is less likely to recur, whether you are on the medication or not. If you have chronic health anxiety, for which medication was providing some benefit, then, when you stop taking it, you might relapse to your previous pattern. For some people (and it is very difficult to predict for whom) the risk of relapse can be minimised by combining the medication with CBT. This can, however, be a two-edged sword. If medication has been very successful in decreasing symptoms of health anxiety, it is quite difficult to learn and practise CBT when you are symptom free! We also don't know what will happen if you have made a good recovery with CBT and you stop taking an SSRI. This is because all the evidence for the high rate of relapse after stopping an SSRI is from people who have taken an SSRI alone, and not when it was combined with CBT. This is where research is required.

Our advice is usually to remain on medication for at least one to two years after recovery. Others would say you may need to be on it for many years. It depends a lot on individual circumstances. If you are planning to stop medication, ensure you do it after discussion with your doctor and within an agreed time frame. Be aware that your health anxiety symptoms may start to return within a few months. If you stop your medication and then recommence it, you may not recover to your previous state. You might want to recommence the same SSRI that helped in the past, but you may now find that you no longer respond to it or that you need a higher dose to obtain the same benefit as before.

If CBT has been unavailable or unsuccessful, you may need to take medication in the long term. As SSRIs have been used for many years without any untoward side effects, experts regard this as quite safe.

Liquid preparations

If you must start your medication at a low dose, then it is usually easier to measure it in liquid form than break a tablet into smaller pieces (where the correct dose cannot be guaranteed). If you are simply unable to tolerate a tablet, then you may find it easier to swallow your medication in liquid form anyway. The drugs available as liquids are listed in Table 12.1.

Use of an SSRI in pregnancy and breastfeeding

SSRIs are generally considered to be safe for pregnant women, as most women taking SSRIs do not report any problems. The benefits and risks of any medication in pregnancy should, however, be discussed in detail with your doctor. A useful resource is the 'Bumps' website www.medicinesinpregnancy.org/

A baby's body and organs are formed during the first twelve weeks of pregnancy. It is mainly during this time that medicines can cause birth defects, though this is rare. While most women taking fluoxetine in pregnancy do not give birth to a baby with a heart defect, an extremely small number do. Sertraline is generally regarded as the safest SSRI for pregnant and breastfeeding women. Most women prefer to treat their health anxiety with CBT alone where pregnancy is possible or planned. However, if you and your doctor believe that medication is necessary, then it is nearly always better for you to be functioning as a mother than suffering from health anxiety.

SSRIs for vegans

Vegans avoid using animal products 'as far as practical and possible'. In most countries, medicines have to pass safety tests before they can be prescribed; and these tests are routinely carried out on animals. Some SSRIs are free of animal products such as gelatin, lactose or stearates. The manufacturers have informed us that citalopram liquid, fluoxetine liquid, clomipramine liquid or paroxetine tablets or liquid do not contain any animal products.

What if I want to stop taking my medication?

If you are already taking medication, please don't stop or change the dose on your own. You may experience symptoms from stopping an SSRI and it's best to reduce such medication slowly. The large majority of people with health anxiety experience mild to no withdrawal symptoms; a very small minority develop marked symptoms that require a more careful reduction of their medication. Withdrawal symptoms can be minimised or prevented if you are pre-warned and manage the situation. Always discuss your wishes with your doctor and plan things together. One of the issues in stopping is trying to assess how much benefit you got from the medication alone (without any therapy). If you derived significant benefit from medication alone, there is a high risk of relapse (e.g. 50 per cent) in the following year. If you do relapse, you can restart the medication, but you may not get the same benefit as before.

Possible withdrawal symptoms can include physical symptoms, for example:

- Flu-like symptoms (aches, fever, sweats, chills, muscle cramps)
- Gastroenteritis-like symptoms (nausea, vomiting, diarrhoea, abdominal pain or cramps)
- Dizziness, spinning, feeling hung over, feeling unsteady
- Headache, tremor
- Sensory abnormalities (numbness, sensations that feel like electric shocks, abnormal visual sensations or smells, tinnitus)

The second group of symptoms that can occur are predominantly psychological, such as depression and anxiety, confusion or feeling detached. However, for the large majority of people with health anxiety, these symptoms are either non-existent or mild. The speed at which stopping a drug causes a symptom is related to how fast the drug is metabolised and removed from your system. Fluoxetine is the least likely SSRI to cause withdrawal symptoms. This is because fluoxetine breaks down very slowly and is in your body for up to five weeks after your last dose. If withdrawal does cause symptoms, they tend to come on within two or three weeks of the last dose. The worst 'offending' drugs for causing withdrawal symptoms are paroxetine (Seroxat; Paxil) which can cause symptoms within the same day as missing the dose. Sertraline (Zoloft) commonly causes withdrawal symptoms within two to three days.

Are my symptoms from stopping an SSRI those of withdrawal or a relapse?

Another problem is deciding whether symptoms are those of *withdrawal* or *relapse* of your health anxiety or depression. The following differences may help you and your doctor to tell:

1. *Did your symptoms come on suddenly or within a week after stopping?*

Withdrawal symptoms come on relatively suddenly within days to weeks of stopping an antidepressant. Symptoms of relapse of health anxiety and depression usually occur within one or two months of stopping.

2. *Are your symptoms physical?*

Withdrawal symptoms that include physical symptoms such as feeling dizzy, light-headed or nauseous, aching as if you have flu, sweating, numbness, electric shocks or headaches, are usually part of a withdrawal state.

3. *How quickly do your symptoms improve when you stop medication?*

Withdrawal symptoms peak within seven to ten days or so and are usually gone within three weeks; by contrast, symptoms of a relapse of health anxiety tend to come on within one to three months. They then tend to persist and may get worse.

4. *How quickly do your symptoms improve if you restart the medication?*

Withdrawal symptoms immediately improve when you restart the drug. Symptoms of relapse may continue or get worse and take several weeks to improve when you recommence an SSRI.

How do my doctor and I reduce the drug slowly enough?

The rate at which you reduce the drug depends (1) on the nature of the drug, (2) the dose you are taking and (3) the severity of any withdrawal symptoms you experience. For example, paroxetine (Seroxat) being prescribed at 20mg daily might be reduced to 15mg or 10mg for two months. Each reduction would then guide the speed at which the medication is further reduced. If withdrawal symptoms emerge then you may have to slow down. For example

- If you experience mild or no symptoms, you need not change the rate of reduction (e.g. paroxetine from 10mg to nothing)
- If you experience moderate withdrawal symptoms, the next reduction would be smaller (for example paroxetine from 10mg to 5mg)
- If you have severe withdrawal symptoms, your doctor may restore the original dose and then start smaller dose reductions (e.g. paroxetine 20mg to 15mg for

a month. If this results in no or mild symptoms, the next step would be to reduce the dose to 12.5mg)

Most withdrawal symptoms can be minimised by reducing the drugs slowly and this should be done under the guidance of your doctor. Some patients have been advised to take the drug on alternate days, but this does not make sense unless it is long-acting drug like fluoxetine.

If SSRI medication doesn't work, is there anything else I can try?

All SSRIs are equally effective overall, but one person may get a better response from one than another. If one SSRI does not work, then best practice is to try a different SSRI in the highest dose you can tolerate for at least twelve weeks. If you have tried an SSRI at the highest tolerated dose and for at least twelve weeks, but your symptoms are not improving, then there are other options. You may be offered a different class of antidepressants e.g. an SSNRI (Selective Serotonergic and Noradrenergic Reuptake Inhibitor) like venlafaxine or duloxetine. This is best discussed with a psychiatrist.

Tranquillisers may be offered by some doctors. These are drugs that aim to reduce anxiety or are sedative. The most common is a group of drugs called benzodiazepines (diazepam or Valium, nitrazepam, lorazepam, clonazepam). Tranquillisers used to be prescribed very commonly in the past but are less used now because of the risks of addiction. They are used for managing severe agitation in depression for the short term. The main side effects are slower reaction times, so they should not be used when operating machinery or driving. The main problem is of dependence, so that a sudden withdrawal can lead to a short-term increase in anxiety, insomnia, irritability, headaches and many other possible symptoms. Withdrawing from such drugs therefore needs to be managed carefully.

13

Seeking help and support

As we mentioned in Chapter 2, when we change our life-style, tackle ingrained habits or recover from an injury it can be helpful to have a person we trust to 'check in' with and discuss progress. Talking to a person who cares enough to engage with your progress can be very helpful in boosting your motivation. It can also be helpful to have a sense that someone is rooting for you, someone who is ready to cheer you on and share in celebrating your successes along the way.

In this chapter, we cover some other sources of support such as charities and professional help.

Charities and support groups

National charities can be an invaluable source of support. They will have information on local resources and support groups. Others can have recommended reading lists and legal advice. Charity support groups may be able to recommend local therapists or psychiatrists. Health anxiety charities can provide a vital forum for people who are new to health anxiety as well as connect sufferers to those who have learned successful ways for coping.

Reading books about health anxiety and doing research on the internet are useful ways of getting further information or support. The more you know about health anxiety and the more you can act as a therapist, then the better equipped you will be to overcome it. And when you recover from health anxiety, you can help raise funds for research into better treatments for health anxiety and campaign for better services by supporting your local health anxiety charity!

Attending a support group

Some people find support groups can be very helpful. Most anxiety support groups just offer general encouragement and information. For some people, attending once is sufficient, as seeing for yourself that you are not alone can be powerful. Other anxiety and phobia groups are set up as 'self-help' groups, where you are expected to report back the following week on the goals you have achieved. It is worth doing your homework on what the format and style of the group is by asking the group leader beforehand so that you can make an informed choice as to whether it's right for you.

If you decide to try a support group, it is important to attend a few sessions and then trust your judgement as to whether it will be helpful for you in the longer term. Groups can change a lot depending on who attends, but when evaluating whether you think the group will help you, try to focus on the group's general culture. Look out for the following:

- Does the group have a culture of being encouraging of people improving and breaking free from their anxiety problems?
- Does the session repeat the same grievances, cycling through the same moans and groans?
- Is the group constructive or do they slip into offering reassurance to each other? It's worth remembering that this can be surprisingly difficult to avoid when you want to help someone feel some relief from their anxiety.
- Rarely they might have a culture of health anxiety being a chronic and untreatable condition. Avoid!

Many groups have ground rules to help avoid these pitfalls; some are run by individuals who are experts by experience and can monitor the group's dynamic. With the right culture, self-help groups (including online support groups) can be a real asset.

Considering professional help

A self-help book can be all that is required for some people with health anxiety. CBT can also be delivered by a computer program over the web. Both of these are more effective if there is a supporter or psychology assistant who is regularly calling you to check on any obstacles and provide encouragement. For many, however, seeing a professional is more effective. This could involve working with a psychologist, psychiatrist or a nurse therapist who is trained in CBT and has experience of treating health anxiety.

Misguided and fraudulent therapists claiming to treat health anxiety exist. This is not meant to scare you; most people with health anxiety who seek professional help will obtain excellent therapy. However, some individuals have described their experience of therapy as ineffective or even counterproductive. If you decide to look for professional help, please keep the following in mind. Only one specific type of psychological therapy has been shown to work for health anxiety and it is called cognitive behavioural therapy.

In choosing a suitable therapist for you, the major danger signs to watch out for are therapists who:

- Do not tell you what type of therapy you are receiving
- Keep asking 'How does that make you feel?'
- Spend *most* of the time wanting you to discuss your childhood or the 'root' cause of your symptoms
- Do not share their understanding of what maintains your health anxiety with you
- Do not problem solve with you
- Teach you 'better' mental compulsions to tell yourself
- Focus only on gradually reducing compulsions without exposure or behavioural experiments
- Find it hard to resist the temptation to reassure you
- Do not negotiate relevant homework between sessions

- Do not monitor your progress in overcoming your symptoms
- Bully or criticise you.

If you are not sure, ask what type of therapy or counselling you are receiving. There is *no* evidence that general counselling, psychodynamic therapy, psychoanalytical therapy, hypnotherapy, mindfulness meditation or transactional analysis are of any benefit in treating health anxiety. People may have found such approaches supportive or helpful for other issues, but they are rarely helpful for overcoming health anxiety. Similarly, beware of any doctor who only offers medication without also recommending CBT without a very good reason (and even then, it would be preferable to have at least a second opinion and assessment by a therapist). This is because if your problems are *severe*, then the combination of CBT and an SSRI may have a better outcome rather than either alone (see Chapter 12).

Fears about seeking help

You may have several worries about seeking help, such as:

- 'What if therapy doesn't help?'
- 'It will be too embarrassing to tell them about my compulsions'
- 'They'll think I'm mad and want to keep me in hospital'
- 'What if they pass the information on to social services or my employer?'

It you find it difficult to talk about some of your thoughts and compulsions, it's usually helpful when seeking help to say you are embarrassed or ashamed. Remember that thoughts about your health are normal and any professional with the slightest experience in health anxiety will be sensitive to your difficulties. They will not consider you mad or want to keep you in hospital against your will. Individuals are only assessed for detention in extreme circumstances such as: if you are a danger to yourself or others or if you are actively suicidal or neglecting yourself badly. What you tell your therapist is kept confidential and cannot be shared with other agencies or your employer without your permission. By law, a therapist can only approach social services or the police in extreme cases when they believe your or another's person life is at risk. You may initially feel that treatment is not helping, but CBT and medication very rarely make health anxiety worse.

In teaching centres, you may be asked if a student or trainee may sit in on your session. If you feel you can, please let them. It is important to continue training more therapists in health anxiety so others can access help. You are of course entitled to refuse. It will never affect your treatment.

Getting the most from CBT

You will get the most from the therapy if you:

- Keep your appointments
- Set goals that you want to achieve and that you can agree on with your therapist

- Are honest and open with your therapist
- Tell your therapist if you feel very embarrassed or ashamed about your symptoms
- Attempt the homework agreed between you and your therapist during therapy sessions. Having a good relationship with your therapist is important but adherence to daily homework is the biggest single predictor of success in therapy
- Act against the way you feel and do the homework you negotiate (at least) daily
- Do the homework even if you are not confident and it makes you uncomfortable. It's important to tolerate the uncertainty and discomfort if you can see that it's in your long-term interest to do so
- Do your homework frequently and for long enough. You can never have too much exposure or too many behavioural experiments!
- Regularly monitor your progress with the therapist by using the rating scales and having clear goals
- Record the sessions so you can listen to them again
- Give the therapist feedback.

Sometimes you may not be ready to work through a CBT plan with your therapist and it may be better to return when you are more committed to change and can do the homework regularly. Don't believe you are a hopeless case. Change, however small, is nearly always possible. When you take a small step, you can build on it. If you have doubts, don't be afraid to seek a second opinion or a referral to a specialist health anxiety centre.

Therapist styles

In CBT, the aim is to have a good, productive, working relationship with your therapist. Some therapists may be more formal in their approach, some might employ more humour. The main thing is that there is a strong foundation of warmth, respect and understanding. A therapist may, at times, need to be firm to help keep your therapy on track and to encourage you to approach things that are difficult. However, this needs to be done with understanding, respect and warmth. There is a big difference between strong encouragement and bullying. You should always feel supported and in control.

Other problems occur when a therapist encourages dependency, maybe telling you that you will need to be in therapy for years. You may be concerned that your therapist seems not to be encouraging you to do enough exposure. You may feel as if you have a somewhat passive therapist who is inactive, inexperienced or lacks credibility. These are important issues to discuss with your therapist. It is not unusual for people to switch therapist or get a second opinion.

Sometimes difficulties in a relationship with a therapist may be related to the way you cope in close relationships. For example, if you feel dependent or angry with your therapist when discussing planned homework, you could be re-enacting an early experience such as with a parent or schoolteacher. We think these issues are generally uncommon in treatment for health anxiety. What no one wants is for you to end up angry or blaming yourself for a breakdown in a relationship when you have an important job to do – that is, focusing your energy on overcoming your health anxiety. If you feel your therapist is negligent or abusive, then of course you must take your complaint to the appropriate professional body.

Complaining

If you want to complain about any professional, think clearly about the nature of the problem – for example, is it the type of treatment, the therapist, the location or something else?

Try to explore whether there might be contributing factors at play. For example, the personality of the therapist may clash with yours. You might be feeling more depressed. Consider if you can sort your complaint out with the therapist themselves or a member of their team. If the professional is refusing further therapy, listen to their reasoning and write down their explanation. If their reasons for denying you further help are to do with limited resources, then don't give up. You may have to persist to get another referral to another provider or there may be an advocate from a charity who can help you.

Types of professionals offering help

There is a range of mental health professionals who will offer help for health anxiety. Most mental health teams are multi-disciplinary, which means that they include people from different professional backgrounds. The following is often confusing for people but it's just the way things are.

- Psychiatrists are medical doctors who specialise in mental disorders. Psychiatrists can prescribe medication for health anxiety and will be more aware of the dose and duration required for health anxiety than your family doctor. Only some psychiatrists are trained in CBT for health anxiety. They may not deliver CBT, but most will be aware of the approach taken and have had experience of CBT in their training.
- Clinical psychologists have a basic training in psychology before specialising in the clinical application of psychological assessment and therapies. They cannot prescribe medication. Many will have had general training in CBT but may not have had specialist training or experience in CBT for health anxiety.
- Counselling psychologists have a basic training in psychology and are then trained in counselling. They cannot prescribe medication. Some have had general training in CBT but have not usually had the specialist training or experience for CBT for health anxiety.
- Nurse therapists were originally trained in psychiatric nursing. A few have trained and specialised in CBT. Most of these will be experienced in treating health anxiety.
- Psychotherapists and counsellors come from a broad range of therapies. Most will listen to you and help you to work through issues in your life. They do not

prescribe medication. They are not usually trained in CBT nor experienced with health anxiety.

It is important to realise that there is nothing to stop anyone calling themselves a counsellor or psychotherapist, whether they are properly trained or not. No therapist with a recognised professional qualification is going to mind you asking about their relevant training and qualifications. It is very important that you satisfy yourself about their accreditation as well as the type of therapy they use and how they learned about health anxiety treatment. Potential questions to ask include: What experience have they got of treating health anxiety (for example the number of patients or clients they have treated)? Are they willing to get their hands dirty in exposure tasks? Will they leave their clinic or use remote video if necessary, to see you in your home or other relevant location? What proportion of their clients/patients have health anxiety and related disorders? What are their expectations for change at the end of therapy and does this match your goals? For some, getting on with their therapist might be the most important quality. If this is important to you, and the professionals you are considering don't have much experience with health anxiety, make sure you connect with a therapist whom you judge to be willing to learn more about your condition.

Finding professional help in the UK

If you would like professional treatment in the UK, your

family doctor is the best place to start. While they may not be particularly knowledgeable about health anxiety, they will usually be aware of what services are available locally. If you are worried about seeing your GP, it can be helpful to take a relative or friend with you. If you find it difficult to talk to your GP, then write them a letter to hand over at the beginning of your appointment. If you doubt that they know about health anxiety, you can always take along information or highlight sections of this book. At your consultation, write down the key questions about local services that you want answered. If you have a significant problem, you can always change your GP. In some areas in England, you may refer yourself for CBT to an IAPT (Improving Access to Psychological Therapies) service, without being referred by your GP. These are listed on the NHS Choices website by searching for IAPT (www.nhs.uk).

The information you tell your GP is confidential and cannot be shared without your permission. In England, you have a right to be referred to a mental health team of your choice (which does not have to be a local team). Communicate clearly that you need cognitive behavioural therapy from a practitioner experienced in health anxiety, and if that means going to a more specialist service, then this is your right. Unfortunately for many public services, you can only be referred to a department and not to a particular individual.

It is usually quicker to obtain help privately, but it does not mean you will necessarily get better treatment. Good and bad treatment can occur both in the public and the private sector. In the UK, you can also try searching for an accredited therapist on the website of the British Association of Behavioural and Cognitive Psychotherapies (www.cbtregisteruk.com). Not all cognitive behavioural therapists choose to become accredited, and many excellent ones are not.

Finding help in the USA

In the USA, finding a cognitive behavioural therapist experienced in health anxiety may also be difficult and depend largely on where you live. You could ask for a referral from your family doctor or recommendation from an academic psychiatry or psychology department. The best recommendation may come from your local health anxiety support group or charities such as the Anxiety Disorders Association of America. Cognitive behavioural therapists are usually members of the Association for the Advancement of Behavioural Therapy who maintain a directory of therapists that can be contacted through their website (www.abct. org).

Finding help in the rest of the world

We have included contact details, in Appendix 1, of other national health anxiety charities around the world that may be valuable resources of recommended professionals dealing with health anxiety.

Appendix 1

International support groups and charities

Australia

Anxiety Recovery Centre Victoria
www.arcvic.org.au

Canada

Alberta OCD Foundation
www.aocdf.com
The Canadian Institute for Obsessive Compulsive Disorders
www.ictoc.org

France

Association Française des personnes souffrant de Troubles
Obsessionnels et Compulsifs
www.aftoc.org

Hong Kong

OCD & Anxiety HK
www.ocdanxietyhk.org

Japan

OCD Ohanashikai
www.ocdsup.net/oha

New Zealand

OCD New Zealand
www.ocd.org.nz

Norway

Norwegian OCD Foundation
www.ananke.no

Singapore

OCD Network Singapore
www.ocdnetworksg.com

South Africa

South African Depression and Anxiety Group
www.sadag.org

UNITED KINGDOM

ANXIETY UK:

W: www.anxietyuk.org.uk
E: support@anxietyuk.org.uk
T: 03444 775774
T: 0300 0772 9844

NO PANIC

W: www.nopanic.org.uk
E: info@nopanic.org.uk
T: 0300 0772 9844

Appendix 2

Forms for exercises

EXERCISE 3.1: PROBLEM LIST

Severity rating: 0–10 (Where 0 is no problem and 10 is very severe)

1 _____

_____

Rating: _____

2 _____

_____

Rating: _____

3 _____

_____

Rating: _____

4 _____

_____

Rating: _____

EXERCISE 3.2: LIST OF GOALS

Progress rating: 0–10 (Where 0 = no progress and 10 = goal completely reached)

SHORT TERM

1 _____ ☐

2 _____ ☐

3 _____ ☐

MEDIUM TERM

1 _____ ☐

2 _____ ☐

3 _____ ☐

LONG TERM

1 _____ ☐

2 _____ ☐

3 _____ ☐

EXERCISE 4.1: UNDERSTANDING YOUR VALUES

Area	Valued direction
1 Intimacy (What is important to you in how you act in an intimate relationship? What sort of partner do you want to be? If you are not involved in a relationship at present, how would you like to act in a relationship?)	
2 Family relationships (What is important to you in how you want to act as a brother/sister; son/daughter; father/mother or parent-in-law? If you are not in contact with some of your family members, would you like to be and how would you act in such a relationship?)	
3 Social relationships (What is important to you in the way you act in the friendships you have? How would you like your friends to remember you? If you have no friends, would you like to have some and what role would you like in a friendship?)	
4 Work (What is important to you in your work? What sort of employee do you want to be? How important to you is what you achieve in your career? What sort of business do you want to run?)	
5 Education and training (What is important to you in your education or training? What sort of student do you want to be? If you are not in education, would you like to be?)	

6 Recreation (What is important to you in what you do to follow any interests, sports or hobbies? If you are not following any interests, what would you ideally like to be pursuing?)	
7 Spirituality (If you are spiritual, what is important to you in the way you want to follow a spiritual path? If you are not, would you like to be and what do you ideally want?)	
8 Voluntary work (What would you like to do for the larger community? For example, voluntary or charity work or political activity?)	
9 Health/physical well-being (What is important to you in how you act for your physical health?)	
10 Mental health (What is important to you generally in how you look after your mental health?)	
11 Any other values that are not listed above	

Source: Adapted from the 'Valued Living Questionnaire', *Acceptance and Commitment Therapy* (Guilford Publications, 2004) by Steven Hayes, Kirk Strosahl and Kelly Wilson.

EXERCISE 7.2: THOUGHT-MONITORING CHART

In the left-hand column note your most common intrusive thoughts and images about your health, and then tick the relevant column (Mon–Sun) each time you have that thought, or add the total from your tally counter.

	Mon	Tues	Wed	Thurs	Fri	Sat	Sun
I have an intrusive thought that							
I have an intrusive thought that							

I have an intrusive thought that	I have an intrusive thought that	I have an intrusive thought image of	I have an intrusive image of

EXERCISE 7.3: ALTERNATIVE EXPLANATIONS

Body sensation	Catastrophic misinterpretation	Possible alternative explanation

APPENDIX 2

EXERCISE 7.4: DESCRIBE THE PROBLEM

Identify the prediction you want to test

_____

_____

_____

Formulate an alternative prediction

_____

_____

_____

Specify how you will test your prediction

_____

_____

_____

Write down the results of your experiment

_____

_____

_____

Analyse the results of your experiment

_____

_____

_____

EXERCISE 7.5: COST-BENEFIT ANALYSIS: REDUCING WORRY

Costs of reducing my worry about my health	Benefits of reducing my worry about my health

Exercise 8.1: Exposure task list

Planned exposure (object, word, place, person, situation, substance)	Anticipated distress 0–100 SUDs (Subjective Units of Distress)

APPENDIX 2

EXPOSURE TASK RECORD SHEET

Exposure task carried out	Level of discomfort	Duration of discomfort	How did you cope?	Testing your expectations	Next steps
Please write out the date and describe what you actually did.	What was your level of anxiety or discomfort on a scale of 0–10 at the start and when it was at its maximum?	How long did the maximum level of discomfort last for?	What helpful things did you do to tolerate your anxiety? Did you use any unhelpful ways of coping (e.g. any checking, reassurance)?	What did you learn about how your problem works? Did your experience strengthen Theory B?	How might you progress from here, e.g. by repeating, extending or developing this exercise, or moving on to an alternative task?
	Start: Maximum:				

Start: Maximum:	Start: Maximum:	Start: Maximum:

EXERCISE 8.2: FREQUENCY OF CHECKING OR REASSURANCE

Date _____

	Mon	Tues	Wed	Thurs	Fri	Sat	Sun

Index

Note: page numbers in italic refer to illustrations or examples. The letter 't' after a page number refers to tables. Where more than one page number is listed against a heading, page numbers in bold indicate significant treatment of a subject.

INDEX